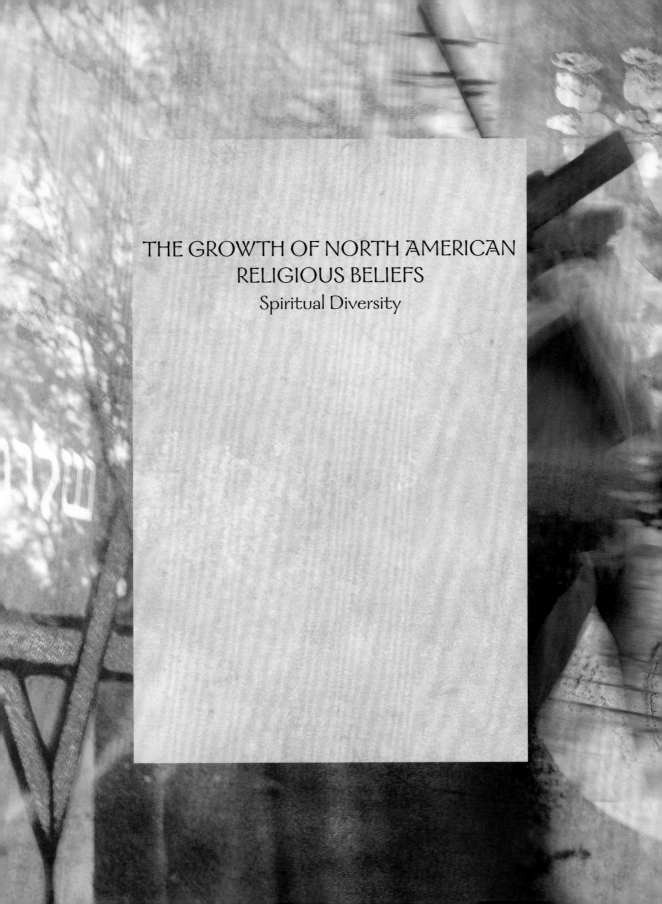

THE GROWTH OF NORTH AMERICAN RELIGIOUS BELIEFS

Spiritual Diversity

RELIGION & MODERN CULTURE
Title List

THE GROWTH OF NORTH AMERICAN RELIGIOUS BELIEFS
Spiritual Diversity

by Kenneth R. McIntosh, M.Div.,
and Jonathan S. McIntosh

Mason Crest Publishers
Philadelphia

Mason Crest Publishers Inc.
370 Reed Road
Broomall, Pennsylvania 19008
(866) MCP-BOOK (toll free)

First printing
1 2 3 4 5 6 7 8 9 10

Library of Congress Cataloging-in-Publication Data

McIntosh, Kenneth, 1959–
  The growth of North American religious beliefs : spiritual diversity /
by Kenneth R. McIntosh and Jonathan S. McIntosh.
     p. cm. — (Religion and modern culture)
  Includes bibliographical references and index.
  ISBN 1-59084-975-2   ISBN 1-59084-970-1 (series)
  1. North America—Religion. I. McIntosh, Jonathan S. II. Title. III.
Series.
  BL2520.M35 2006
  200'.973—dc22
                                        2005015371

Produced by Harding House Publishing Service, Inc.
www.hardinghousepages.com
Interior design by Dianne Hodack.
Cover design by MK Bassett-Harvey.
Printed in India.

CONTENTS

INTRODUCTION

by Dr. Marcus J. Borg

You are about to begin an important and exciting experience: the study of modern religion. Knowing about religion—and religions—is vital for understanding our neighbors, whether they live down the street or across the globe.

Despite the modern trend toward religious doubt, most of the world's population continues to be religious. Of the approximately six billion people alive today, around two billion are Christians, one billion are Muslims, 800 million are Hindus, and 400 million are Buddhists. Smaller numbers are Sikhs, Shinto, Confucian, Taoist, Jewish, and indigenous religions.

Religion plays an especially important role in North America. The United States is the most religious country in the Western world: about 80 percent of Americans say that religion is "important" or "very important" to them. Around 95 percent say they believe in God. These figures are very different in Europe, where the percentages are much smaller. Canada is "in between": the figures are lower than for the United States, but significantly higher than in Europe. In Canada, 68 percent of citizens say religion is of "high importance," and 81 percent believe in God or a higher being.

The United States is largely Christian. Around 80 percent describe themselves as Christian. In Canada, professing Christians are 77 percent of the population. But religious diversity is growing. According to Harvard scholar Diana Eck's recent book *A New Religious America*, the United States has recently become the most religiously diverse country in the world. Canada is also a country of great religious variety.

Fifty years ago, religious diversity in the United States meant Protestants, Catholics, and Jews, but since the 1960s, immigration from Asia, the Middle East, and Africa has dramatically increased the number of people practicing other religions. There are now about six million Muslims, four million Buddhists, and a million Hindus in the United States. To compare these figures to two historically important Protestant denominations in the United States, about 3.5 million are Presbyterians and 2.5 million are Episcopalians. There are more Buddhists in the United States than either of these denominations, and as many Muslims as the two denominations combined. This means that knowing about other religions is not just knowing about people in other parts of the world—but about knowing people in our schools, workplaces, and neighborhoods.

Moreover, religious diversity does not simply exist between religions. It is found within Christianity itself:

• There are many different forms of Christian worship. They range from Quaker silence to contemporary worship with rock music to traditional liturgical worship among Catholics and Episcopalians to Pentecostal enthusiasm and speaking in tongues.

- Christians are divided about the importance of an afterlife. For some, the next life—a paradise beyond death—is their primary motive for being Christian. For other Christians, the afterlife does not matter nearly as much. Instead, a relationship with God that transforms our lives this side of death is the primary motive.
- Christians are divided about the Bible. Some are biblical literalists who believe that the Bible is to be interpreted literally and factually as the inerrant revelation of God, true in every respect and true for all time. Other Christians understand the Bible more symbolically as the witness of two ancient communities—biblical Israel and early Christianity—to their life with God.

Christians are also divided about the role of religion in public life. Some understand "separation of church and state" to mean "separation of religion and politics." Other Christians seek to bring Christian values into public life. Some (commonly called "the Christian Right") are concerned with public policy issues such as abortion, prayer in schools, marriage as only heterosexual, and pornography. Still other Christians name the central public policy issues as American imperialism, war, economic injustice, racism, health care, and so forth. For the first group, values are primarily concerned with individual behavior. For the second group, values are also concerned with group behavior and social systems. The study of religion in North America involves not only becoming aware of other religions but also becoming aware of differences within Christianity itself. Such study can help us to understand people with different convictions and practices.

And there is one more reason why such study is important and exciting: religions deal with the largest questions of life. These questions are intellectual, moral, and personal. Most centrally, they are:

- What is real? The religions of the world agree that "the real" is more than the space-time world of matter and energy.
- How then shall we live?
- How can we be "in touch" with "the real"? How can we connect with it and become more deeply centered in it?

This series will put you in touch with other ways of seeing reality and how to live.

THE OPPORTUNITIES & CHALLENGES OF RELIGIOUS DIVERSITY

It's OK if you're a Muslim,

it's OK if you're a Jew,

*it's OK if you're **agnostic***

and you don't know what to do,

have a merry

Chrismahanakwanzaka to you.

This song from a Virgin Mobile television ad, which aired December 2004, was funny, catchy, and different from all the commercials aired during holiday seasons of the past. The ad included persons of every race and both genders. It portrayed people of all religions as well—from an Orthodox Jew on the piano to Hindu dancers. At the very end of the commercial, a low voice said, "And ***Pagans*** too!"

This commercial clearly reflected the changing religious reality of North America. No longer is it fashionable to wish everyone "Merry Christmas!" or even, "Merry Christmas and Happy Hanukkah!" In the twenty-first century, Canadians and U.S. citizens celebrate Christmas, Hanukkah, Kwanza, Ramadan, Winter Solstice, or no religious holidays at all—depending on their faith and cultural background. So, it is either "Happy Holidays" or "Happy Chrismahanakwanzaka!"

RELIGIOUS DIVERSITY IN NORTH AMERICA TODAY

The Virgin Mobile commercial reflects enormous changes that have occurred in the North American religious scene over the past forty years. Until the 1950s, many people thought of the United States and Canada as "Christian" nations, or "Judeo-Christian" nations. But there were other religions in North America at the time. Native spiritual beliefs existed on the continent before Europeans arrived, and Africans brought their ancestral faith with them on the slave ships; whites forced people of color to give up their spiritual practices. Those who continued to observe these religions did so mostly in secret. On the surface, Christianity appeared to be America's religion.

Today, the United States and Canada are clearly a spiritual smorgasbord with a varied religious menu serving people of all different cultures and faiths. This is evident just driving through the cities of the United States and Canada. Churches with crosses on their steeples still dominate the old downtown sections of cities, but now Buddhist temples dot Toronto, a magnificent Hindu temple with elephants on its walls graces a Nashville, Tennessee, suburb, and a new Islamic center covers a corner in Johnson City, New York. Places of worship for people of various faiths are being constructed in cities across North America.

GLOSSARY

agnostic: Someone who believes that it is impossible to know whether God exists.

civil rights: Rights that all of a society's citizens are supposed to have.

ecumenical: Involving or promoting friendly relations between different religions.

humanist: Someone who follows a doctrine or way of life centered on human interests or values rather than a supernatural authority.

Jains: Those who practice Jainism, an ancient branch of Hinduism that rejects the idea of a supreme being and advocates a deep respect for living things.

Pagans: Those who do not follow one of the world's main religions, especially somebody who is not a Christian, Muslim, or Jew, but instead follow one of the Earth religions, where the Goddess is often emphasized.

Pentecostal: Relating to any Christian denomination that emphasizes the workings of the Holy Spirit, interprets the Bible literally, and adopts an informal demonstrative approach to religious worship.

radical: Having to do with an extreme, often quick desire for change.

Santeria: A religion that combines West African Yoruba religion with Roman Catholicism.

Sikhs: Members of a religious group that broke away from Hinduism during the sixteenth century and advocated belief in only one God, with some aspects of Islam.

Wiccans: Those who practice Wicca, a religion involving nature-worship; some Wiccans call themselves witches, but they do not worship the devil.

Zoroastrians: Those who practice Zoroastrianism, an ancient religion founded in Persia with the principal beliefs that there is a supreme being and a cosmic contest between two spirits, one good and one evil.

RELIGION & MODERN CULTURE

"Different religions can engage in dialogue with one another. . . . If they really believe that there are valuable elements in each other's tradition and that they can learn from one another, they will also discover many valuable aspects of their own tradition through such encounter. Peace will be a beautiful flower blooming on this field of practice."

—*Thich Nhat Hanh, Buddhist monk*

According to Diana Eck, professor of Comparative Religion at Harvard University and director of the Pluralism Project, "The United States is . . . now the most profusely religious nation on earth." Muslims in the United States outnumber Episcopalians and Presbyterians. Los Angeles has more varieties of Buddhism than any city in the world, and across the United States, there may be as many as four million Buddhists. More than a million immigrants from India worship the many facets of deity in Hindu home shrines and local temples. Counting religious adherents is difficult, and numbers given in religious surveys are notoriously inaccurate. Some estimates are much lower, but the big picture is clear—America is a land of great spiritual variety.

Canada is also changing rapidly in terms of religion. In 1901, only 2 percent of Canadians claimed a non-Christian religion. In 2001, that jumped to almost 30 percent. In a 2001 census, almost eight million Canadians—16 percent of the population—claimed to be of "no religion," and less than one in five Canadians goes to religious gatherings during any given week. Canadians who consider themselves agnostic, atheist, *humanist*, or simply of no religion make up the second-largest religious group in the country. Christians in Canada are declining at a

THE OPPORTUNITIES & CHALLENGES
OF RELIGIOUS DIVERSITY

13

rate of one percentage point each year. At the same time, non-Christian religions in Canada are growing. If these trends continue, Christians will become a minority in Canada by 2023. During the first decade of the twenty-first century, there are almost 600,000 Muslims in Canada. Meanwhile, the number of **Wiccans** and Pagans increased 281 percent between 1991 and 2001, the fastest percentage growth of any religious group in the country, though their absolute numbers remain small. Native people who say they follow the traditional beliefs of their cultures also have increased dramatically in number in recent years.

THE ORIGINS OF RELIGIOUS DIVERSITY

In the United States, the First Amendment to the Constitution guarantees that the government shall not establish or prohibit the exercise of religion. This ensures that no religious group in the nation can legally "squeeze out" any other religious group. Although the United States has seen its share of religious prejudice—and it still does today—the nation's laws safeguard each person's right to worship as he or she pleases. The Founding Fathers of the United States would doubtless be surprised to see the great variety of religions practiced by Americans today, but they intended to create a country offering equal protection to religious choices of every kind.

On July 4, 1965, President Lyndon Baines Johnson sat at the base of the Statue of Liberty and signed a new immigration law. The 1965 Immigration and Naturalization Act was the result of a new concern for **civil rights** in America. As U.S. citizens became more aware of the evils of racism, they also realized that former immigration laws had kept out people of color from other nations.

The 1965 immigration act has changed the shape of America—and America's religions. Since 1965, almost a million immigrants a year

THE OPPORTUNITIES & CHALLENGES
OF RELIGIOUS DIVERSITY

15

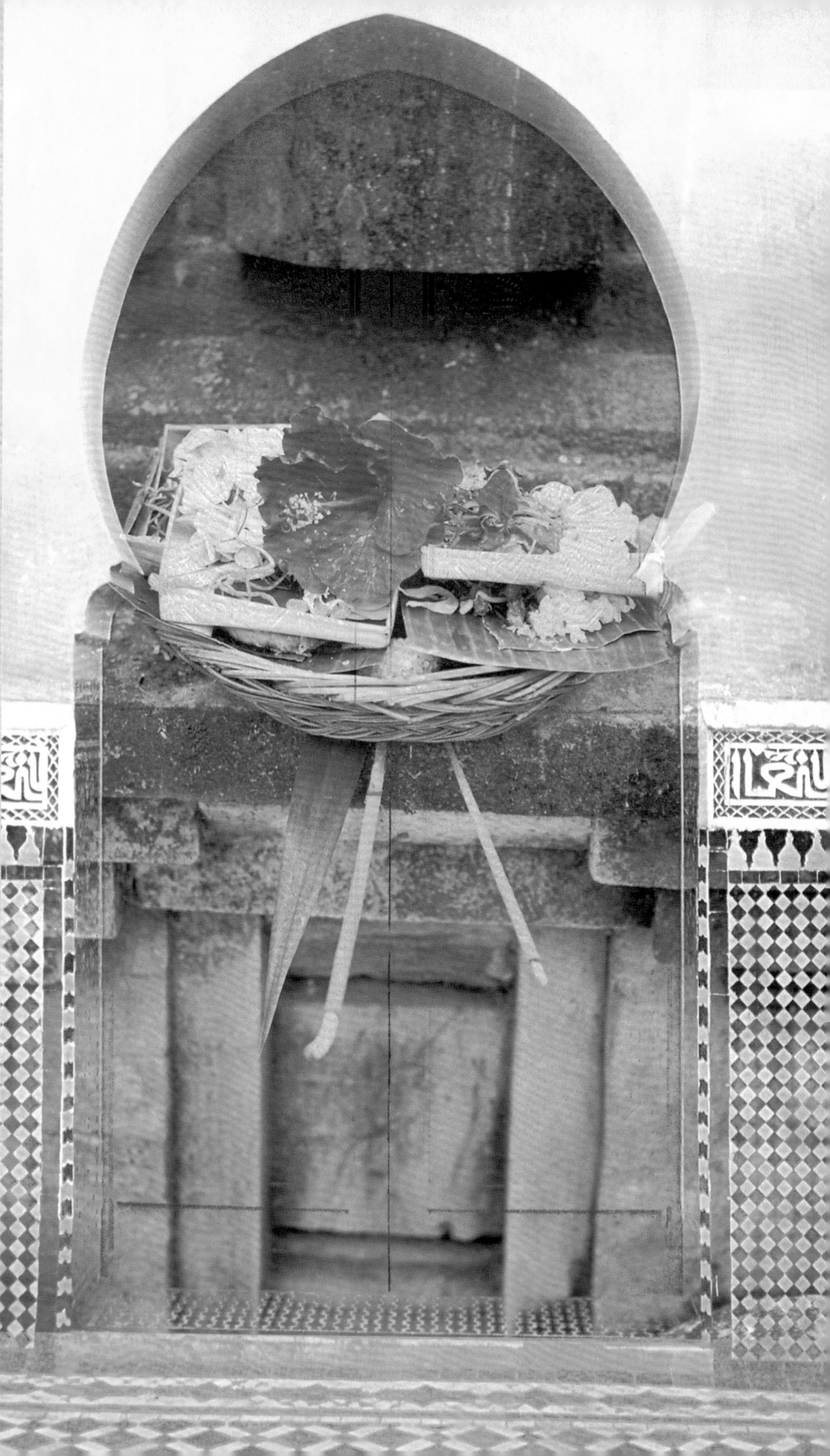

"Tolerance implies no lack of commitment to one's own beliefs. Rather, it condemns the oppression or persecution of others."

—*President John F. Kennedy*

have come to live in the United States. From Thailand, Vietnam, Cambodia, China, and Korea, Buddhists have come. Hindus have arrived at America's shores from India, East Africa, and Trinidad. Followers of Islam have come from Indonesia, Bangladesh, Pakistan, the Middle East, and Nigeria. From India, the United States has received **Sikhs** and **Jains**; from India and Iran, **Zoroastrians**. Practitioners of **Santeria**, combining Roman Catholicism and West African ancestral religions, have come from Cuba. Jewish refugees have arrived from the former Soviet nations. Latin American immigrants bring their Roman Catholic and **Pentecostal** beliefs. In short, immigration has filled America's plate with a wonderful mix of spiritual beliefs.

America's religious diversity is not entirely due to immigration, however. Along with changes in law, the 1960s brought changes in attitudes. Young people were experimenting with everything—communal living, psychedelic drugs, sexual freedom, and new religions. Encouraged by **radical** authors, musical celebrities, and traveling spiritual leaders, the children of the '60s revolution in Canada and the United States began investigating Buddhism and other religions. For some, it was just a phase, but others, like actor Richard Gere, became lifelong followers of these spiritual traditions.

Today, some religions in North America—such as Hinduism—are still largely immigrant religions. Most American Hindus have come from India, or are children of Indian immigrants. However, a large percentage of Buddhists in the United States are descendants of Europeans who claimed Christian beliefs when they arrived in the New World long ago. Buddhism is no longer an exclusively "Eastern" religion. The attitude of freedom and experimentation that began during the cultural revolution of the 1960s continues to encourage the religious diversity we see in the United States and Canada today.

THREE DIFFERENT RESPONSES TO DIVERSITY

Citizens have taken three different approaches to religious diversity. One approach is exclusivism. This approach attempts to keep differing forms of belief away from the rest of the "Christian" United States. Prior to the 1960s, various immigration laws attempted to limit the immigration of certain races or cultures into the United States; that was a legal attempt at exclusivism. Religious hate crimes—against either people or their property—are the most vicious forms of exclusivism. When members of a religion are not allowed to purchase property for a house of worship, that action can be an expression of exclusivism as well.

Assimilation is another possible response to diversity. Assimilation is the attempt to change people's beliefs and practices, making them conform to the ways of the majority population. This idea is contained in the old expression that America is a "melting pot." That assumes other ethnic groups' cultural distinctions melt down and dissolve so that Americans are all similar. For more than a century, for example, government agencies in the United States and Canada removed Native children from their homes and sent them to boarding schools. They punished the children for speaking their tribal languages or practicing the spiritual ways of their people. This was a blatant attempt to assimilate indigenous people into European cultures and belief systems.

The most positive response to religious diversity is pluralism. Pluralism means more than just diversity. Diversity is recognition that there are many varieties of religions. Pluralism goes beyond recognition and affirms, "We understand and appreciate our differences." Pluralism is the active attempt by people of differing beliefs and cultures to learn

THE GIRL SCOUTS HAVE GOT IT

Girl Scouts in the twenty-first century do a whole lot more than just sell cookies. They encourage respect for diversity and preservation of each scout's cultural heritage. The organization has drafted an excellent definition of pluralism:

> Diversity and pluralism are not the same, and although you can have diversity without pluralism, you cannot have pluralism without valuing diversity. Diversity can simply mean counting the variety of people. Pluralism means that we value people for the variety they bring to the group.

about one another, to share lives and ideas. The goal of pluralism is a society with diversity that promotes understanding and the exchange of ideas between differing groups.

THE OPPORTUNITIES OF RELIGIOUS PLURALISM

Many citizens see wonderful opportunity in North America's religious diversity. In the past, North Americans would read books, or take college courses, or travel abroad in order to learn about "world religions."

Many were curious about different cultures and beliefs, but it was not easy to learn about them. Today, what used to be called "world religions" are American religions.

Shortly after the tragedy of the World Trade Center attacks, many Christian Americans were talking about Muslims. Obviously, they had more questions than answers. Many Christians wanted to learn more about what Muslims really believe. Decades ago, they might have gone to the library to get a book, or tried to find a professor of Eastern religions at a college. Instead, some Americans got on the phone and called the local Islamic Center. Instead of merely learning about Islam, Americans who did this were able to do something better: form relationships with human beings who lived Islam. They could learn about the Muslim faith from the tone of people's voices and the gleams in their eyes. They could ask questions, and ask them again if they did not understand something. America's religious diversity offers all its citizens opportunities for this sort of valuable learning experience.

Pluralism does not mean one must give up her own beliefs in order to appreciate others. That would be assimilation. In a pluralistic society, a Hindu remains a Hindu, a Christian remains a Christian, and an atheist remains an atheist—each one proud to follow her own form of faith. At the same time, in a pluralistic society the Hindu, the Christian, and the atheist each understands the others' beliefs and recognizes them as part of the mosaic that is America today.

Diana Eck describes her perspective as a Christian who follows the Methodist tradition: "Through the years, I have found my own faith not threatened but broadened by the study of Hindu, Buddhist, Muslim, and Sikh traditions of faith."

NEGATIVE REACTIONS TO RELIGIOUS PLURALISM

In May 1997, a discussion took place on the South Carolina state board of education concerning the display of the Ten Commandments. When the issue of religious diversity entered the discussion, one public official

21

RELIGION & MODERN CULTURE

said, "Screw the Buddhists and kill the Muslims." It was an ironic comment when discussing a set of laws that includes "You shall not kill" and "You shall not bear false witness against your neighbor." Widespread outcry arose against the remarks, but the official remained on the state board of education.

Supporters might say this comment was "only words," but words can incite people to terrible actions. In the past several years, dozens of violent attacks were motivated by religious hatred. In June 2000, for example, a man with a shotgun opened fire on Muslim worshippers entering their mosque in Memphis, Tennessee. On September 17, 2001, in Black Mesa, Arizona, police charged a man with first-degree murder in connection with a series of shootings. Police said the shootings were a racially motivated response to the terrorist attacks on New York and Washington. Police charged Francisco Roque with shooting Balbir Singh Sodhi, a Chevron gas station owner and immigrant from India; the Indian's turban made him look like an Arab. Over the past decade, vandals and arsonists have damaged synagogues, Buddhist temples, and Muslim mosques in apparent religious hate crimes.

In the summer of 2000, the Palos Heights, Illinois, city council offered prospective buyers $200,000 to withdraw their bid on a piece of property. The property was a former Christian Reformed Church building. Local Muslims who wished to build an Islamic center on the site were the potential buyers. During heated public discussions, one city official described Islam as "an upside down religion." Others, including the former pastor of the Reformed Church, were adamant that their community should model freedom of religion for all. They felt Palos Heights would be a better community with the Islamic center. In the end, the Muslims chose not to buy the site. (The Muslims originally accepted the cash payment, but in July 2000, the city's mayor vetoed the payment offer.) They did not want to go where some members of the community did not want them. Similar scenarios have taken place in other U.S. communities. Disallowing houses of worship can be a legal form of discrimination against religious minorities.

While some individuals have reacted to religious diversity with hostility, many individuals and groups have worked to encourage religious pluralism in the United States and in Canada. Most large North American cities have interfaith coalitions or *ecumenical* roundtable groups. These organizations regularly bring together members of different religious groups—often clergy and scholars—to share and discuss their diverse spiritual beliefs.

Businesses have made changes to accommodate the varying spiritual lives of their members. In the United States, Title VII of the Civil Rights Act of 1964 prohibits employers from discriminating based on employees' religion. It requires employers to make "reasonable accommodation" for the religious needs of workers, at least as long as this does not impose "undue hardship" on the employer.

In Denver, Colorado, approximately a hundred Muslim cab drivers pick up people and drop them off at the Denver airport. Since followers of Islam must kneel and pray five times a day, Muslim taxi drivers at the Denver airport were inconvenienced during cold winter weather. They asked if the city could help them. The City of Denver responded by building a glass prayer shelter near the airport, where the taxi drivers could pray to Allah more comfortably. Jillian Lloyd of the *Christian Science Monitor* noted, "The move highlighted the growing willingness of American employers to provide for their workers' religious needs."

The U.S. military has also been noted for its receptivity to religious pluralism. Like the rest of the U.S. government, the services cannot establish or promote one religion over another. At the same time, they are committed to providing chaplains for each different religious group represented in the services. In the late 1990s, Fort Hood, Texas, the nation's largest military base, made headlines for having a Wiccan chaplain. When the army named Marcy Palmer, High Priestess for Wiccans

on the base, "soldier of the year," an officer at Fort Hood received an un-
happy phone call from a Roman Catholic woman asking, "Do you mean
to tell me the Department of Defense recognizes Wicca?" The officer
replied, "It may come as a shock to you, Madam, that the Department of
Defense does not recognize the Roman Catholic Church." The Armed
Forces recognize no religions officially, but they try to meet the spiritual needs for soldiers of all different religions.

25

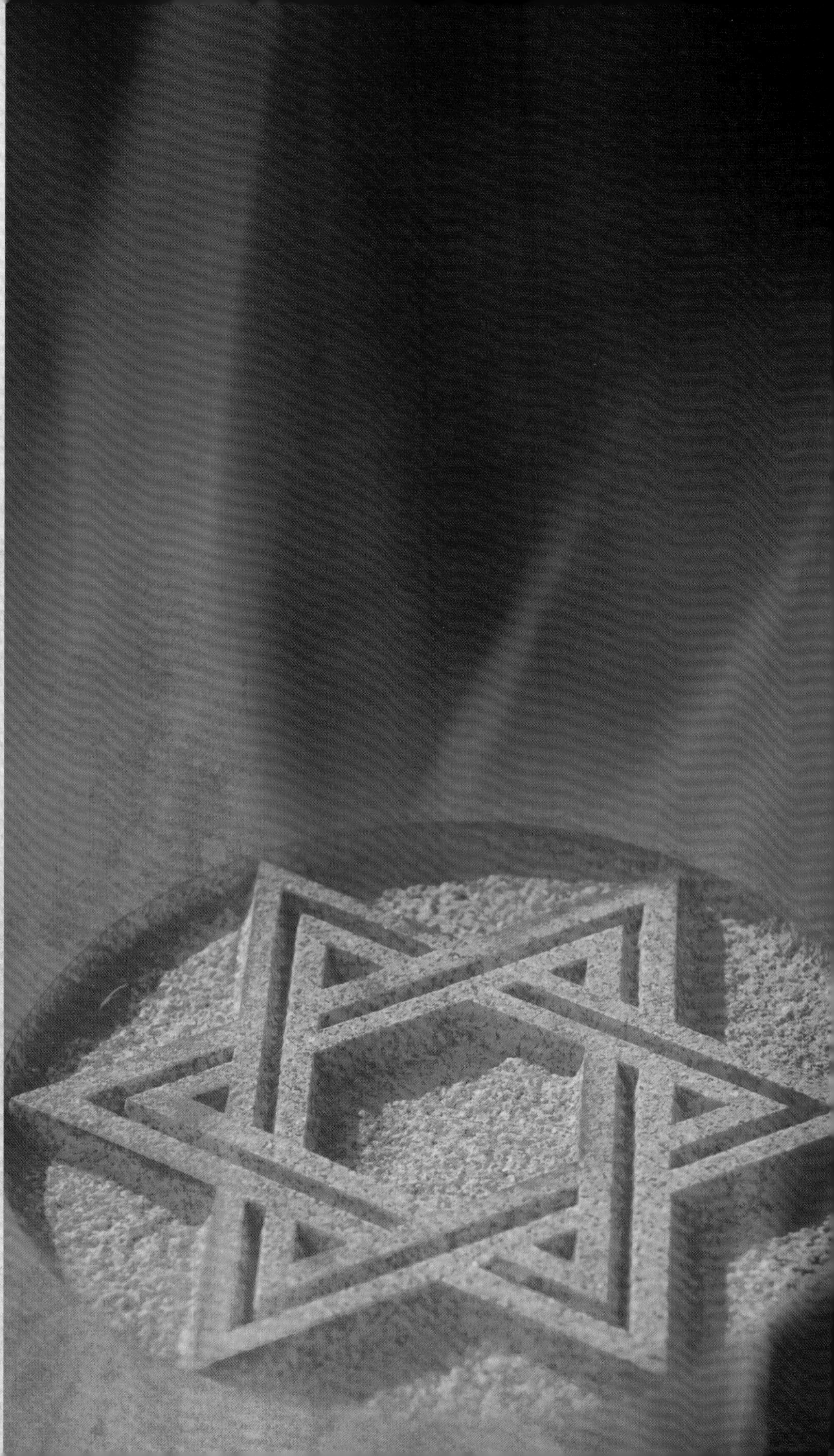

FROM EVIL, GOOD

Most religions teach that the deity is able, mysteriously, to bring forth good outcomes even when people do evil things. This has happened repeatedly in cases where hatred against a religion has led to entire communities working harder to embrace religious pluralism.

On the tragic morning of June 18, 1999, arsonists burned three synagogues in Sacramento, California. The oldest Jewish congregation west of the Mississippi River lost its library of more than five thousand books in the fire. Members of the synagogues were shocked. They asked, "How could this happen in America? What have we done? Why do they hate us so much?"

As horrible as this incident was, it also brought forth unexpected expressions of sympathy from the rest of the Sacramento community. The Muslim Public Affairs Council released a statement that "People of all faiths must band together to reject the intolerance demonstrated by this violent act." Services took place the following Sabbath in a local theater. Eighteen hundred people from the Sacramento area—Catholics, Protestants, Buddhists, and Hindus—came from the community to display solidarity with their Jewish neighbors. In the midst of the service, the Reverend Faith Whitmore from a local United Methodist church addressed the gathered worshippers: "I want you to know that this afternoon we took a special offering of our members to help you rebuild your temple, and we want you to have this check for six thousand dollars." There were a few moments of silence, followed by thunderous applause. Though the Sacramento arsons were actions of hatred and prejudice, they brought forth an unprecedented display of support for the Jewish community from people of different faiths.

Chapter 2

RELIGION & MODERN CULTURE

CHRISTIANITY & JUDAISM IN NORTH AMERICA

On April 18, 1993, St. Paul's United Methodist Church and the Islamic Society of the East Bay in Fremont, California, broke ground together for a new church and a new mosque, to be built side by side. Six hundred people were there.... The two communities mingled in an atmosphere of celebration.... They named the new frontage road that enters their property Peace Terrace.

Diana L. Eck relates this story in her book *A New Religious America*. Both the Muslims and the Methodists were looking for a suitable site to build new houses of worship. They met each other at a meeting, when two adjacent lots became available.

They realized they could each get more out of their properties if they shared a common parking lot. They also understood they would accomplish more by going to city hall together and voicing their common concerns with one voice. Furthermore, by working together, they hoped to set a positive example of religious cooperation. Now completed, the dome of the mosque and steeple of the Methodist church stand side by side, sending a message to the Fremont community—"Muslims and Christians are next-door neighbors."

Christianity is still the largest religion in North America. However, it is grappling with newly diverse spiritual realities. The Fremont Methodist congregation's partnership with their Muslim neighbors is just one of many ways North American Christians are adjusting to the complex picture of twenty-first century religious diversity.

OVERVIEW: CHRISTIANITY IN NORTH AMERICA

At the start of the twenty-first century, Christianity is still the faith with the largest numbers of followers in North America, and Judaism may remain the second-largest faith group (though by some counts Islam has numbers similar to Judaism). Again, it is very difficult to get accurate numbers regarding religions. One estimate says there are 159 million Christians in the United States, as of 2001. (The total U.S. population is 293 million.) In Canada, approximately 21 million of Canada's 29 million citizens consider themselves Christian. At the same time, only 30 percent of Canadians said personal religion is important to them. In the United States, almost twice that number—59 percent—regard religion as personally important.

Roman Catholics are the largest single group of Christians in North America. In Canada, there are 12.8 million Catholics, or 43 percent of the population. According to 2003 estimates, there are approximately 51 million Catholics in the United States. Today's Catholic Church

GLOSSARY

Baha'i: A religion founded in Iran in 1863 that maintains that the teachings of all religions are of value, believes humankind is spiritually one, and advocates peace.

Charismatics: Members of Christian groups or worship characterized by a quest for inspired and ecstatic experiences.

liberal: More accepting of differences, open to new ideas.

secular: Not controlled by a religious body or concerned with religious or spiritual matters.

stereotypes: Standardized ideas held by one person or group about another person or group, often incorrect and based on incomplete information.

Talmud: A body of Jewish tradition regarded as authoritative.

Torah: Jewish scripture consisting of the five books of Moses (also referred to as the Pentateuch).

claims its beliefs and practices come from the original universal (that is, catholic) church. Bishops lead the Church. Foremost among them is the pope, who also serves as representative for the entire Church. Roman Catholic spirituality focuses on the sacraments, rituals that communicate the presence of Christ to believers.

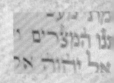

Evangelicals are also influential in North America—both in numbers and in influence through the media. It is difficult to determine the number of evangelicals in North America, as evangelicalism is a matter of individual belief, rather than membership in a certain kind of church. Estimates vary greatly, but there may be 24 million evangelical Christians in the United States. A 2001 survey suggests 780,000 evangelicals in Canada.

Evangelical Christians emphasize a personal relationship with God, entered into by an internal experience of "accepting Jesus Christ as Savior." They teach that a person must "ask Christ into his heart," thus becoming "born again" and beginning a new way of life. Evangelicals regard the Bible as the inspired Word of God, and encourage study of the scriptures. They believe God wants them to share this "Good News" (Gospel) with others both by word and deed. Informal prayer—talking to God about everyday needs—is also an important part of evangelical spirituality.

Evangelicals have been highly visible in North American popular culture during the start of the twenty-first century. Pastor Rick Warren, for example, of California's enormous Saddleback Church, sold 20 million copies of his book *The Purpose Driven Life*. Evangelical novelists Tim LaHaye and Jerry Jenkins have sold more than 62 million books in their popular *Left Behind* series. These books are based on a particular evangelical interpretation of the book of Revelation (see the Mason Crest book *Prophecies and End-Time Speculations: The Shape of Things to Come* for a detailed explanation).

Protestant mainline denominations—long-established church groups such as the Methodists, Lutherans, Episcopalians, and Presbyterians—are also part of the North American religious scene. In Canada, there are two million Anglicans and over half a million members of other mainline Protestant churches. In the United States, there are fourteen million Methodists, nine million Lutherans, and five million Presbyterians. Members of mainline Protestant churches vary in

CHRISTIANITY & JUDAISM IN NORTH AMERICA

במר ו בוע-
תי המצרים י
אל יהוה אל

34

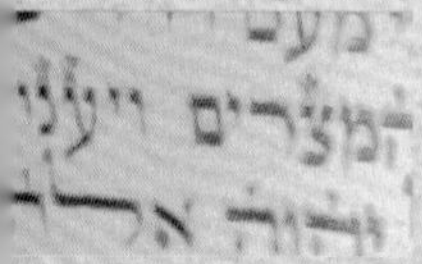

RELIGION & MODERN CULTURE

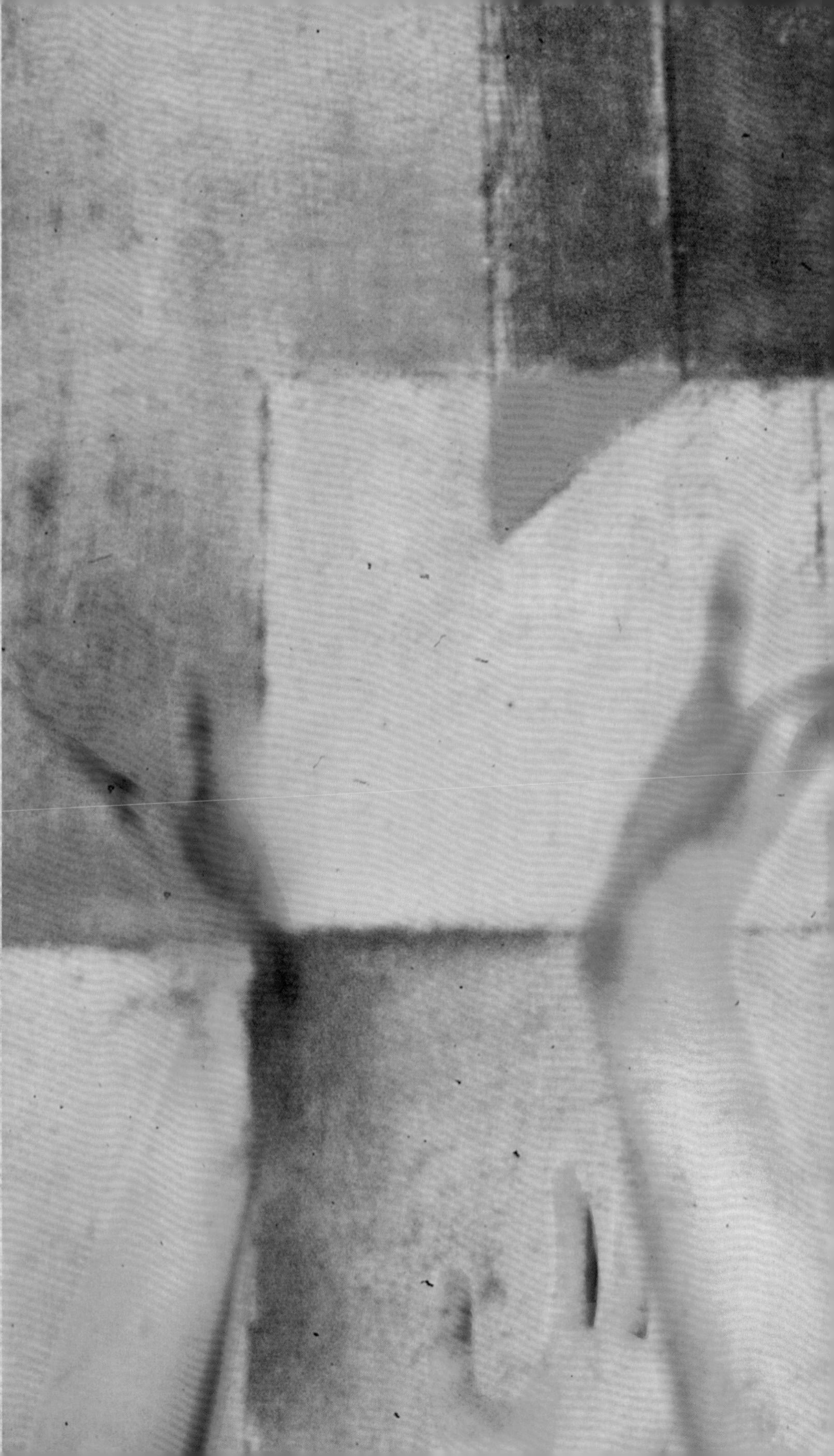

"When an alien lives with you in your land, do not mistreat him. . . . Love him as yourself, for you were aliens in Egypt. I am the Lord your God."

—*from Leviticus 19*

their understanding of Christian faith. Some are evangelical in their faith; others have more *liberal* views regarding the Bible and spiritual life.

Is Christianity in North America gaining or declining in membership? Again, the numbers reported by different surveys vary. In Canada, all Christian groups reported decline between 1991 and 2001. Presbyterians had the worst losses, a 36 percent decline. The most positive report came from the Anglicans, who lost only 7 percent of their members during the same time. Pentecostals and *Charismatics*—who have grown in numbers worldwide—lost 15 percent of their members during the past decade in Canada. This contrasts with figures for Pentecostals and Charismatics in the United States, where their numbers have increased.

Christian groups in the United States are either holding even or losing numbers, depending on which survey one reads. The most positive report on U.S. Christian churches' overall membership suggests a slight increase between 1991 and 2001. Gains in U.S. Christian churches during the past few years came mostly from immigration. Asian immigrants have formed thousands of evangelical and Pentecostal churches in U.S. cities. The Latino population in the United States has also swelled in recent years, and surveys show Latinos are strongly religious. Approximately one of three Hispanics is Pentecostal, and most of the remainder is Roman Catholic. The Latino influx has transformed many Catholic parishes.

Other recent reports suggest that Christianity in the United States is declining at a rate similar to that in Canada. According to the

"There are people who do not accept the full Christian doctrine about Christ but who are so strongly attracted by Him that they are His in a much deeper sense than they themselves understand. There are people in other religions who are being led by God's secret influence to concentrate on those parts of their religion which are in agreement with Christianity, and who thus belong to Christ without knowing it."

—*C. S. Lewis, famous Christian philosopher of the last century, in his book* Mere Christianity

American Religious Identification Survey by the Graduate Center of the City University of New York, "The proportion of the [U.S.] population that can be classified as Christian has declined from 86% in 1990 to 77% in 2001." In one of the most negative reports, a January 2002 *USA Today*/Gallup Poll showed that almost half of American adults appear to be alienated from organized religion. The study suggests that if current trends continue, most adults will not call themselves religious within a few years. Rodney Stark, a professor of sociology at the University of Washington and a coauthor of *Acts of Faith: Explaining the Human Side of Religion*, differs with that view. According to Professor Stark, the numbers leaving churches are not necessarily opposed to religion. He says, "People who believe in God—and they do—who pray—and they do—are not **secular**, they are just unchurched. They've never been to church and, in many cases, their parents didn't go either." Perhaps one can say that America is not becoming less spiritual, just less "religious."

The largest drop in North American Christianity may be coming in the next few decades. One survey of U.S. churches suggests that three

LATTER-DAY SAINTS

The Mormon Church is also significant in the United States. The Church of Jesus Christ of Latter-Day Saints (LDS), known informally as the Mormons, is one of the fastest-growing religions in the world. In the United States, there are almost five million Mormons. Numbers in Canada are much lower, with 151,000 members. Young volunteer missionaries aggressively recruit for the LDS Church. Mormons differ from other groups who follow Christ in that they regard the *Book of Mormon*, which came out in the nineteenth century, as another testament of Jesus Christ, equal in authority to the Bible.

out of four elderly attend church, one out of two middle-aged people attend church, but only one out of five adults younger than thirty go to church. If this is the case, the number of people who attend church will drop rapidly in the next twenty years.

While Christian numbers in the United States are static or declining, other religions are seeing notable increases. From 1991 to 2001, Islam has doubled; Buddhism has grown 170 percent; those following Native American spiritual traditions have also doubled. Some smaller groups, such as Wiccans, Pagans, Sikhs, and *Baha'i*, have gained adherents in excess of 200 percent between 1991 and 2001.

RELIGION & MODERN CULTURE

REACTIONS FROM CHRISTIANS TO RELIGIOUS DIVERSITY

Christian clergy and scholars hold diverse views regarding whether believers in other faiths share a common eternal destiny. These varying beliefs in turn shape Christian responses to religious diversity.

The Roman Catholic Church holds that non-Catholic religions are "gravely deficient." At the same time, they believe God's kindness reaches out to people of other religions (or even people who claim no religion). God "enlightens them in a way which is accommodated to their spiritual . . . situation." Thus, Catholics desire to see others become Catholic, but also believe members of other religions may share in a common salvation in eternity.

Some evangelicals believe there is "no other name besides Jesus" by which mortals attain salvation. Thus, only those who have a personal relationship with God by explicitly confessing faith in Christ will reach heaven. Other evangelicals say that all persons who come to heaven will do so because of the accomplishments of Christ on their behalf, but they do not have to be consciously aware of that. In this view, God considers the amount of spiritual knowledge and the hidden intentions of the heart in each human being—and rewards them accordingly. Finally, a smaller number of evangelicals believe in after-death conversion. In this view, many who follow different spiritual beliefs in life will become Christians in the next life.

Many mainstream Protestants embrace religious pluralism in their theology. Diana Eck, who identifies herself as "a Christian, a Montana-born, lifelong Methodist," says, "I have found that only as a Christian pluralist could I be faithful to the mystery and presence of the one I call God. Being a Christian pluralist means daring to encounter people of very different faith traditions and defining my faith not by its borders, but by its roots." In his book *The Heart of Christianity*, popular author and Jesus scholar Marcus Borg writes, "I am convinced . . . that God

39

. . . is known in all major religious traditions. Indeed, if I thought I had to believe that Christianity was the only way, I could not be Christian." He concludes, "We can sing our love songs to Jesus with wild abandon without having to demean other religions."

JUDAISM IN NORTH AMERICA TODAY

Before today's explosion of American religions, many regarded Judaism as North America's other major religion. There are approximately three million Jewish believers in the United States, and 360,000 in Canada. The number of Jewish believers in Canada has declined slightly over the past decade, while in the United States, the number has gone down by 10 percent from 1991 to 2001.

Judaism in North America is very diverse. Orthodox Jews dress distinctively and attempt to follow the commandments of the Hebrew Bible to the letter. The largest group of synagogues, Reformed Judaism, views the Bible more liberally. Reformed Judaism emphasizes personal morality over rituals or exact observance of ancient biblical laws. Those affiliated with Conservative Judaism follow the **Torah** and **Talmud**, but make allowances for changing times. A significant number of North American Jews do not attend synagogue, yet celebrate their Jewish heritage in personally meaningful ways.

Judaism teaches that people of all religions will have a place in the world to come. Jews believe Christians and Muslims worship the same Creator who will reward all mortals according to their moral behavior, and Jews do not seek to convert non-Jews to their religion. In fact, according to traditional teachings, rabbis should try three times to convince those who wish to convert to stay with their own religions. Thus, Judaism does not see religious pluralism as a threat or a call to convert others. At the same time, however, many North American rabbis work

hard to encourage people in their congregations to keep their Jewish customs. They appreciate their distinct role in America's spiritual diversity.

Christianity and Judaism are familiar to most citizens of the United States and Canada, even if those citizens do not follow these religions. Music, art, and literature reflect Jewish and Christian influences. Islam is less well known in North America, even though it has a notable history on this continent. Many men and women hold *stereotypes* and misunderstandings of Islam. The Muslim faith is growing quickly in the United States and Canada, and North Americans need to understand this religion that is based on knowing and doing the will of God.

Chapter 3

RELIGION & MODERN CULTURE

NORTH AMERICAN ISLAM

June 25, 1991, marked an important mile-
stone in American religious history, although few U.S. citizens took note of it. For
the first time, a Muslim religious leader offered prayer as chaplain for the U.S. House
of Representatives. The man who prayed
that morning was Siraj Wahaj, an African
American ***imam*** from Brooklyn, New York.
His mosque, Masjid al-Taqwa, had transformed a rundown, crime-ridden section of
the neighborhood into a vibrant, positive
community. Imam Wahaj offered his prayer
on a Muslim holy day, *Eid al-Adha*, which
commemorates Abraham's faithfulness to
God in his willingness to sacrifice his son
Ishmael.

Imam Wahaj prayed:

In the name of God, Most Gracious, Most Merciful. Praise belongs to Thee alone; O God, Lord and Creator of all the worlds. Praise belongs to Thee who shaped us and colored us black and white, brown, red, and yellow. Praise belongs to Thee who created us males and females and made us into nations and tribes that we may know each other.

His prayer echoed a passage from the *Qur'an*, affirming that Allah (the Arabic word for God, the word used by Jewish and Christian Arabs as well) created a diversity of people with the desire that they know and understand each other. In the twenty-first century, an increasing number of North Americans are becoming familiar with their Muslim neighbors. There are as many as five to six million followers of Islam in the United States, outnumbering Presbyterians, Episcopalians, and Mormons. Furthermore, they number more than Quakers, Unitarians, Seventh-Day Adventists, Mennonites, Jehovah's Witnesses, and Christian Scientists combined. Some surveys show Islam has overtaken Judaism as the country's second-largest religion. In Canada, there are 580,000 Muslims, making Islam Canada's largest non-Christian religion.

Many people wrongly assume that most American Muslims are primarily Middle Eastern. In fact, less than one out of eight American Muslims (12.4 percent) are of Arab descent. The two largest Muslim groups in the United States are native-born blacks (42 percent) and immigrants from South Asia (24 percent). Furthermore, there are increasing numbers of converts from mainstream American culture.

GLOSSARY

imam: A man who leads the prayers in a mosque.

Qur'an: The sacred text of Islam, believed by Muslims to record the revelations of God to Mohammad; also spelled Koran.

HISTORY OF ISLAM ABROAD & IN THE UNITED STATES

The Arabic word "Islam" means "surrender" or "submit"; to practice Islam is to submit to the will of God. A person who follows this way is a Muslim—in Arabic, "one who submits" to God. The Prophet Mohammed, born in 571 CE in the city of Mecca, in Arabia, founded Islam. When Mohammed was forty, he claimed that God gave him revelations that showed him the way of submission to Allah. Followers of Mohammed wrote down his revelations and compiled them in the book called the Qur'an. Later, other sayings were collected in another work called the Hadith. After the prophet's death, Islam split into two branches, Sunnis and Shiites. Their beliefs are similar, but the division came about over disagreement regarding the prophet's successor.

Islam has similarities to both Judaism and Christianity. It is strongly monotheistic—believing in only one God. Muslims regard Abraham as

DATING SYSTEMS & THEIR MEANING

You might be accustomed to seeing dates expressed with the abbreviations BC or AD, as in the year 1000 BC or the year AD 1900. For centuries, this dating system has been the most common in the Western world. However, since BC and AD are based on Christianity (BC stands for Before Christ and AD stands for *anno Domini*, Latin for "in the year of our Lord"), many people now prefer to use abbreviations that people from all religions can be comfortable using. The abbreviations BCE (meaning Before Common Era) and CE (meaning Common Era) mark time in the same way (for example, 1000 BC is the same year as 1000 BCE, and AD 1900 is the same year as 1900 CE), but BCE and CE do not have the same religious overtones as BC and AD.

the first great prophet. They also respect Moses and Jesus. They teach that Jesus was born of the Virgin Mary and believe he will return at the Last Judgment. Unlike Judaism and Christianity, Islam views Mohammed as the last and greatest of the prophets. Moreover, the Qur'an explicitly states that Jesus was not divine (whereas Christians believe he was).

In the eighteenth and nineteenth centuries, slavers brought West Africans to the United States by force to serve as slaves. Doubtless, many of them continued to believe in Islam and secretly followed its beliefs. However, this was difficult, as owners punished slaves brutally for observing their African cultural ways. A century after gaining their freedom, many blacks in America would rediscover their ancestors' Islamic faith.

At the very end of the nineteenth century, immigrants from modern-day Jordan and Lebanon came to the United States. Most of these immigrants planned to work in America for less than a decade and return to their homes wealthier than when they left. However, they appreciated and enjoyed the ideals of their new country and many remained in North America.

Muslims call the mosque in Cedar Rapids, Iowa, "the Mother Mosque of North America." Muslims began worshiping in Cedar Rapids in 1895; in 1929, they appointed their first imam; and in 1935 began construction of the building, which became known simply as "the Muslim Temple." Cedar Rapids residents probably did not expect that believers in Allah and Mohammad would build other mosques in virtually every mid-sized American city. Today there are more than 1,400 mosques in the United States and Canada. Eighty percent of these began after 1980.

At the same time that Muslims of Arabic ancestry established their faith in North America, a revival of Islam began among African Americans as well. In the 1930s, Nobel Drew Ali established the Moorish Science Temple of Islam, a religion for blacks in America. At the beginning, their scripture was the Holy Koran of the Moorish Science Temple of America, a book that is not the same as the Qur'an revealed by Mohammad. After Ali, Wallace D. Fard and then Elijah Muhammad led the Moorish Science Temple, which ultimately became known as the Nation of Islam. The Nation of Islam emphasizes black pride and claims Fard and Elijah Muhammad as Allah's prophets.

From 1952 to 1965, the Nation of Islam became famous because of Malcolm X, its charismatic national representative, one of the most eloquent and forceful representatives for black pride during the civil rights era. In 1964, Malcolm X made the hajj, the pilgrimage to Mecca that

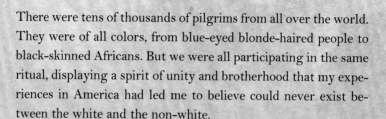

Muslims from around the world attempt to make at least once during their lifetime. There, he had a powerful experience. As he described it:

> There were tens of thousands of pilgrims from all over the world. They were of all colors, from blue-eyed blonde-haired people to black-skinned Africans. But we were all participating in the same ritual, displaying a spirit of unity and brotherhood that my experiences in America had led me to believe could never exist between the white and the non-white.

Because of this experience, Malcolm X was determined to change the direction of the Nation of Islam; he wanted to bring it into union with the rest of the Muslim world. After the assassination of Malcolm X, W. D. Muhammad, son of Elijah Muhammad, led the majority of black Muslims. Like Malcolm, he yearned for a religion that would include people of all races, where "All will be Muslims. All children of God."

PILLARS OF ISLAM

Five essential practices are required of all faithful Muslims. These are the Shahada (confession of faith), prayer, fasting, giving charity, and making the hajj.

The words of the Shahada are: "I bear witness that there is no God but Allah, and Mohammed is a prophet of God." When a person says these words with heartfelt conviction, she becomes part of Islam. Joanne Richards is one person who recently chose to do this. Born and raised in California, Richards' teen years were full of trouble. Then she met a young Muslim man who impressed her spiritually, and he influenced her to get—and read—a copy of the Qur'an. She says, "What most impressed me was the forgiveness and mercy. That incredible Graciousness of Allah. I was going to need lots of these blessings with the kind of life I was living." Joanne Richards admits it has not been

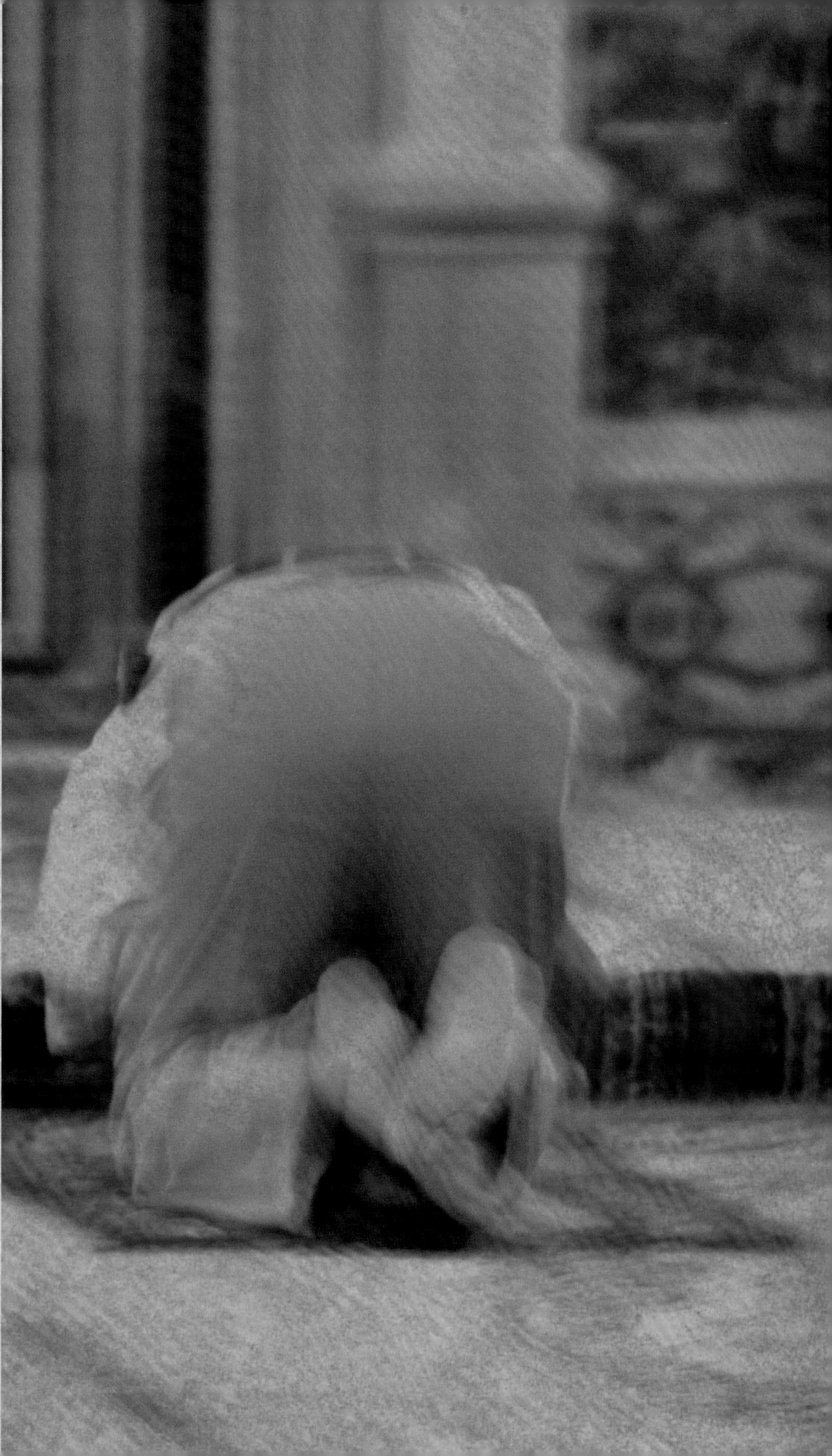

entirely easy fitting into her new faith. As a single woman from a non-Muslim background, she is unusual. Despite the difficulties, she says, "For me, embracing Islam has been the single greatest gift ever granted to me."

Prayer (*Salat*) is observed five times daily: just before daybreak, at noon, in the middle of the afternoon, just after sunset, and after dark. In Middle Eastern nations, one can hear the call to prayer broadcast from towers attached to mosques. In the United States, the call to prayer is announced at the Islamic Center in Washington, D.C.; on Joy Road in Detroit, Michigan; and on Divisadero Street in downtown San Francisco. Most Muslims in North America, however, must set their own prayer schedule. It has become common for American employers and schools to provide breaks and room for Muslims to observe Salat.

Muslims fast (go without food or eat very little) during Ramadan. According to Ramadan on the Net:

> Ramadan is the ninth month of the Muslim calendar. The Month of Ramadan is also when it is believed the Holy Qur'an was sent down from heaven. . . . Ramadan is a time when Muslims concentrate on their faith and spend less time on the concerns of their everyday lives. It is a time of worship and contemplation. During the Fast of Ramadan, strict restraints are placed on the daily lives of Muslims. They are not allowed to eat or drink during the daylight hours.

In *A New Religious America*, Diana Eck tells of a Muslim college girl named Najeeba who was dreading Ramadan. She was the only Muslim she knew at her small college, and she feared that observing the fast would emphasize how different she was from the other students. The first morning of Ramadan, she went to the cafeteria before sunup so she

"In the name of Allah, Most Gracious, Most Merciful. Praise be to Allah, the cherisher and sustainer of the worlds; Most Gracious, Most Merciful; Master of the Day of Judgment, Thee do we worship, and Thine aid we seek, Show us the straight way."

—*The opening words of the Holy Qur'an*

could eat before the fast began. She was pleasantly surprised to find a group of her friends already awake and waiting for her. Some of them shared the ritual of fasting through the day; others joined her again for supper after sundown. None of her friends was Muslim, but they showed their friendship by providing her with company during the month of fasting.

Zakat is the spiritual practice of giving charity. It may be directed to a mosque or to needy persons. Numerous Islamic agencies based all over the world distribute Zakat. They help Muslims in war-ravaged countries such as Chechnya, Bosnia, Afghanistan, Kashmir, Sudan, Bangladesh, and Turkey. Zakat arrives in the form of schools, hospitals, food, and shelter.

Faithful Muslims are obligated at least once during their lifetime to make the hajj. That means approximately one-fifth of the people on earth attempt to travel at least once to this place they regard as most holy. Each year, some two million people journey to Mecca for this pilgrimage. Michael Wolf, an ABC journalist and convert to Islam who made the hajj in 1998, described his experience: "Here I join people from all over the earth, all these human beings drawn together by the call of an idea, by the oneness of God."

THE FRUIT OF ISLAM

The Nation of Islam is known for its unarmed and highly disciplined corps of volunteers, "the Fruit of Islam." They have protested and shut down drug houses in poor neighborhoods, and they have made such a good reputation for security that they have been hired to patrol high-crime areas in America's big cities. Furthermore, their clean appearance, fine manners, and powerful sense of self-respect have made them models for urban youth, adding more luster to their religion.

SOME MISUNDERSTOOD PRACTICES

Although there are great numbers of Islamic believers in North America, many U.S. and Canadian citizens continue to stereotype and misunderstand the Muslim faith. The most serious misunderstanding involves the concept of jihad. Jihad literally means "struggle," and unfortunately many North Americans first heard the term in connection with tragic incidences of terrorism by Muslim fanatics targeting their non-Islamic Middle East neighbors and Westerners.

Jihad refers to actions undertaken to defend or promote Islam. If Muslims are attacked, jihad does include actions of warfare used to defend the faith. It can also include getting an Islamic education and

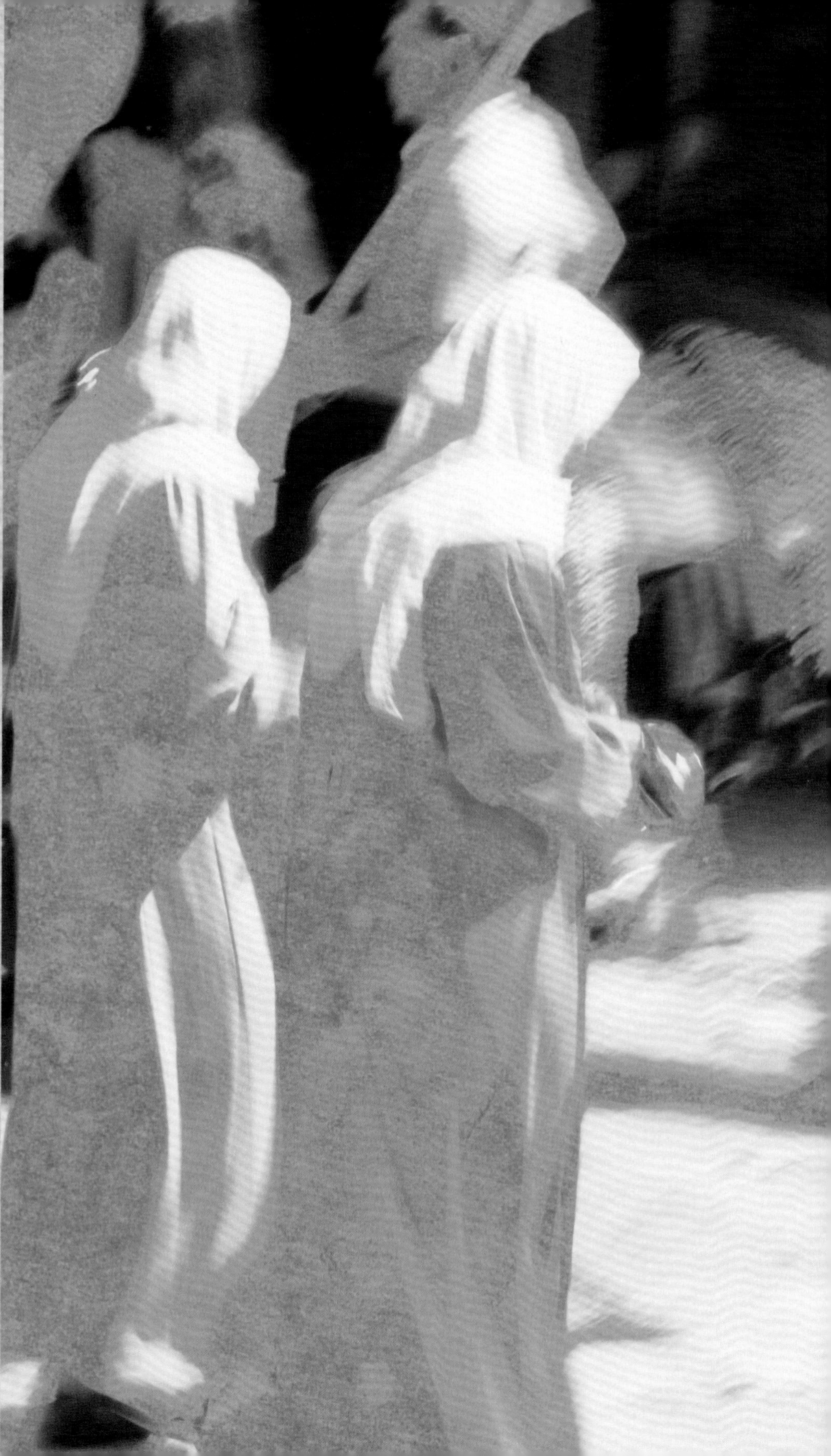

*"Be steadfast in prayer; Practice regular charity;
and bow down your heads with those who bow
down in worship"*

—*Surah 2:43 from the Holy Qur'an*

speaking or writing to promote Islam. There is also the "inner jihad," sometimes called "the Greater Jihad." This is the struggle that takes place within each believer to submit his or her will to Allah. In other words, inner jihad is spiritual self-control.

Islamic teachers point out that terrorism is conducted by only a very few Muslims. The Qur'an forbids self-destruction and harm to civilians in warfare. Furthermore, war is to be conducted primarily for purposes of self-defense. Imams sometimes say that terrorists are to Islam what the Ku Klux Klan is to Christianity—a few people whose hateful fanaticism separates them from the overwhelming majority of believers in their religion.

North Americans also often misunderstand the practice of women's head covering, or *hijab*. Many Muslim women, both in North America and in progressive Muslim nations like Jordan, choose not to wear the hijab. At the same time, for many Muslims in the United States and Canada, the veil is an important way to express their spiritual identity. Fariha Khan, a teen in Rockville, Maryland, says, "To me, hijab is a gift from Allah. It gives me the opportunity to become closer to Allah. Also quite importantly, [it provides me] the chance to stand and be recognized as a Muslim."

Islam, Christianity, and Judaism share some common understandings of God, moral commandments, and the importance of written scriptures. Buddhism differs markedly from these monotheistic religions. At the same time, the *Dharma* (path or direction) of the Buddha appeals to increasing numbers of people in the twenty-first century.

Chapter 4

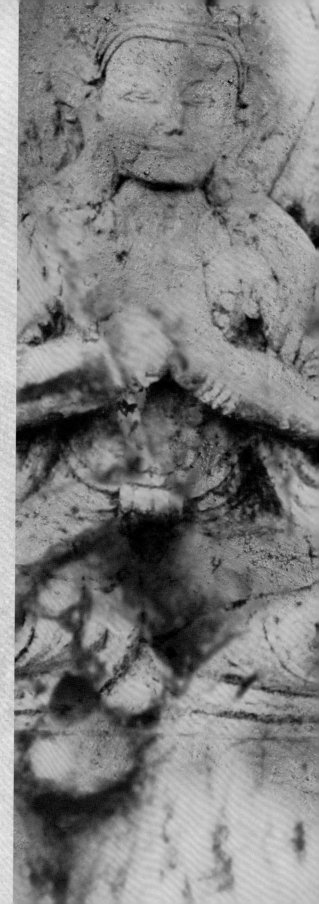

NORTH AMERICAN
BUDDHISM

RELIGION & MODERN CULTURE

In late July 1996, an unusual gathering took place at Gethsemani Abbey in Trappist, Kentucky. At this Roman Catholic monastery, where monks of the Benedictine religious order have lived for more than a century, a delegation of Catholic monks and nuns from all over the United States met with a delegation of Buddhist spiritual leaders. The Buddhist group included the world-renowned Dalai Lama, the Venerable Mahaghosananda, known as "the Gandhi of Cambodia," and spiritual leaders from seven different nations.

The gathering was the most significant exchange in history between Buddhists and Christians. They did not spend too much time discussing religious theories, however. Most of their discussion focused on practical issues of the religious life: "How do we deal with anger?" "How do we experience genuine compassion for others?" Both Christian and Buddhist participants at the meeting had experienced persecution, and they were able to sympathize with each other's sufferings. In *A New Religious America*, Diana Eck summarized the meeting: "The sense of communion between Christian and Buddhist *monastics* here ran deep. Religious communities, even monastic communities, may have many differences, but in the depths of the spiritual life, there are simply no borders."

More than three decades before the meeting, two monks—one Christian and one Buddhist—planted the seeds that grew into this exchange. Thomas Merton, a Benedictine monk from Gethsemani Abbey famous for his writings on the spiritual life, and Thich Nhat Hanh, a Vietnamese Buddhist monk known for his efforts at peacemaking, formed a friendship and ongoing discussion about their lives. The major event that grew from their friendship, decades later, signaled the growing importance of Buddhism in the United States in recent years.

Scholars estimate there may be as many as four million Buddhists in the United States. Of these, almost a million are "nonethnic" Buddhists—that is, converts to Buddhism from Western cultural backgrounds. There are approximately eight hundred Buddhist spiritual communities in the United States, ranging from teaching centers to monasteries. In Canada, there are some 300,000 Buddhists and dozens of Buddhist spiritual communities.

While the U.S. Buddhist population is smaller than those of the Christians, Jews, and Muslims, it is nevertheless growing at an amazing rate. Its numbers have increased tenfold since 1960. If Buddhism in the United States continues to grow at even half that rate, there will be fifteen to twenty million Buddhists by 2035. In Los Angeles alone, there are more than three hundred Buddhist temples, monasteries, and schools. The Hsi Lai Buddhist temple in Hacienda Heights, California,

monastics: Those, especially monks, who live with others in a monastery and observe religious vows.

has more than 20,000 members. It is as large as any Christian church in the country. A number of popular Buddhist publications are produced monthly in the United States, including *Tricycle*, with 50,000 subscribers, and *Shambhala Sun*.

U.S. celebrities have helped promote Buddhism in North America. Actor Richard Gere, for example, follows Tibetan Buddhism and has appeared with the Dalai Lama. Jazz musician Herbie Hancock and singers Tina Turner and Bonnie Raitt are all Buddhists. While some Buddhists are concerned that celebrities foster a "pop" image of the Dharma, the religion's popularity among this group is also a sign that Buddhism has been widely accepted in North America.

SHAKYAMUNI BUDDHA
& THE MAJOR BRANCHES OF BUDDHIST FAITH

The Sanskrit word *buddha* means "awakened one." Since it refers to a person who has achieved spiritual illumination, all persons are potential buddhas. The man referred to as the Buddha was born in 566 BCE in what is now Nepal. His family name was Guatama, and his personal

name was Siddhartha. He is also known as Shakyamuni, "the sage from Shakya clan." Buddhists do not regard Shakyamuni Buddha as a god, a special form of spiritual being, or a prophet. He was a human being like others who one day woke up to the fullness of spiritual reality.

In May of 531 BCE, Shakyamuni Buddha sat beneath a fig tree in deep meditation. While doing this, he attained an extraordinary state of enlightenment, or spiritual knowledge. He said, "Now the bonds of ignorance and craving are sundered, deliverance is obtained for all! All living beings are buddhas, endowed with wisdom and virtue!" After achieving enlightenment, the Buddha possessed the "Dharma." These are the important teachings that would define Buddhism for centuries.

In the centuries following Guatama Buddha's life, those who followed the Dharma separated into three distinct traditions: Theravada, Mahayana, and Vajrayna. The rituals and emphases of the various branches of Buddhism differ, but they share the same basic beliefs.

HOW THE DHARMA CAME TO NORTH AMERICA

The word "Buddhism" did not appear in an English-language dictionary until 1812. Henry David Thoreau translated the *Lotus Sutra* in the 1840s, the first English translation of any Buddhist work. After that time, Thoreau referred to "my Buddha" as central to his religious beliefs.

While living in Japan, American businessperson William Bigelow converted to Buddhism in 1885. He later returned to his home in Boston, Massachusetts, where he struggled for years with a lack of spiritual support for his newfound beliefs.

In 1893, the World's Parliament of Religions met in Chicago, Illinois. Most of the delegates assumed the parliament would show the superiority of Christianity to the more "primitive" religions of the world. In fact, this event gave Buddhism its first significant exposure in

"I take refuge in the Buddha,
The one who shows me the way in this life.
I take refuge in the Dharma,
The way of understanding and love.
I take refuge in the Sangha,
The community that lives in harmony
and awareness."

—*Thich Nhat Hanh*

the West—and began its influence on North America. Dharmapala from Sri Lanka delivered a speech titled "The World's Debt to Buddha," in which he asserted that Buddhism contained many "Christian" virtues and predated Christianity by five centuries. Soyen Shaku, a Japanese Zen Master who also spoke in Chicago, tried to show how Buddhism was compatible with many of the new "scientific" understandings then popular in America. The American public enthusiastically received both Dharmapala and Shaku.

After the Parliament of Religions, Dharmapala was asked to travel and lecture about Buddhism throughout the United States. The first night in New York, Charles T. Strauss, a New Yorker of Jewish background, came up to speak with Dharmapala after the meeting. Strauss asked if he could become Buddhist and affirmed his commitment to the Buddha, the Dharma, and the Sangha. He thus became the first American to confess faith in Buddhism, according to the appropriate ritual, on American soil. In the next century, almost a million of Strauss's fellow citizens would follow in his steps.

The twentieth century saw successive waves of Japanese, Chinese, Cambodian, and Thai immigrants arrive in the United States. By the end of the century, these immigrants added some three million Buddhists to America's spiritual diversity. During World War II,

"Radiate your loving kindness to every living being without discrimination."

—*The Buddha*

Japanese American Buddhist leaders had to suffer in concentration camps, along with their flocks, but that did not dampen their faith.

In the 1950s, several famous American authors became attracted to Buddhism. Jack Kerouac became familiar with Buddhism through reading Thoreau's *Lotus Sutra* and other translations of Buddhist works. Beat poet Alan Ginsberg became aware of Zen Buddhism first through reading library books, then by contact with the First Zen Institute of America. Around the same time, an Episcopal priest named Alan Watts began practicing Buddhism. In 1957, Watts published an influential book titled *The Way of Zen*. These outstanding literary artists made Buddhism popular with the American public just before the cultural revolution of the 1960s, which in turn helped Eastern religions come to full bloom in the United States.

THE THREE TREASURES OF BUDDHISM

When a person formally accepts Buddhism, he says, "I take refuge in the Buddha, the Dharma, and the Sangha." The Buddha refers to Shakyamuni Buddha and the examples he set with his life. The Dharma are his teachings, as they are passed down in the living traditions of Buddhism. The Sangha means "spiritual community." That could be a Buddhist temple, monastery, or school. These are referred to as "the three treasures of Buddhism."

When a Buddhist says "I take refuge in the Buddha," that is different from an evangelical Christian saying "I accept Christ." Unlike the way Christians regard Christ, Buddhists emphatically do not regard Shakyamuni Buddha as God or a god. According to ancient tradition,

BUDDHIST FAITH DURING INTERNMENT

Bishop Matsukage of the Japanese Jodo Shinshu School spent World War II in an internment camp, serving the needs of his fellow Buddhists. After the war, Matsukage remained excited about the future of Buddhism in the United States. He wrote his own epitaph, which relatives later engraved on his tombstone:

Bury My ashes
In the Soil of America
And into Eternity,
May the Dharma prosper!

two travelers came upon Shakyamuni Buddha and were awestruck by his appearance. They asked him, "Are you a heavenly being? A God? An Angel?" He replied, "No, I am awake." Buddhism teaches that every person has a "buddha nature"—that is, the capability to become spiritually enlightened, or awake. The Buddha is important because he showed the way for others to awaken their own buddha nature.

The Dharma is composed of the many teachings of the Buddha and of his followers. Unlike the Christian Bible and Jewish Torah, Buddhists do not regard the Dharma as a particular written text or even a set of texts. The Dharma is "the path" set forth in Buddhist teachings and, more important, in Buddhist lives. In his book *Living Buddha, Living*

65

RELIGION & MODERN CULTURE

Christ, Thich Nhat Hanh writes, "When those who represent a spiritual tradition embody the essence of their tradition, just the way they walk, sit and smile speaks volumes about the tradition." In other words, beliefs may be important, but they are irrelevant if people merely talk about rather than experience them.

The Sangha is spiritual community. The spiritual teachers say that one cannot truly practice Buddhism if she attempts to do so alone. Books and videos do not by themselves a Buddhist make. Living humans help one "catch" enlightenment. In the East, the Sangha was usually a monastery. There are Buddhist monasteries now in America, but the Sangha in the United States is more likely to be a teaching center.

In 1959, Shunryu Suzuki came from Japan to America to teach Zen meditation to Japanese Americans living in San Francisco. Soon after he arrived, he found many American students from the larger community asking for instruction in meditation. They seemed more interested than did Suzuki's fellow Japanese. To see if they were serious, Suzuki told these spiritual seekers he would teach them meditation at 5:30 each morning. To his surprise, they showed up and carefully followed his instructions. Seeing the public demand, Suzuki established the Zen Center of San Francisco, which continues to be influential.

Whatever form it takes, participation in a Sangha is vital for Buddhist practice. Bernard Tetsugen Glassman, one of America's noted Zen teachers, writes in *A New Religious America*, "It's a little bit like joining an orchestra. It's much easier for you to get in tune when you're part of that group than if you're just by yourself."

THE FOUR NOBLE TRUTHS

When he achieved enlightenment, Shakyamuni Buddha began to teach the Four Noble Truths—the core principles for illumination. The first noble truth is: "Life is suffering." That may seem like a hard pill to

swallow for Americans who are just as happy to say, "Don't worry—be happy." However, the first Noble Truth communicates well with spiritual seekers who have experienced harsh realities. Sylvia Boorstein, a Jewish-Buddhist meditation teacher, describes her first encounter with the first Noble Truth:

What a relief it was for me to go to my first meditation retreat and hear people speak the truth so clearly—the first Noble Truth that life is difficult and painful, just by its very nature, not because we're doing it wrong. I thought to myself, "Here are people . . . who know the truth and are willing to name it and are all right with it."

The second Noble Truth says: "There is a cause of suffering—our desires and attachments to things, trying to hold onto things as if they were unchanging in a world where everything changes and passes away." Sylvia Boorstein explains:

From this point of view, there is a big difference between pain and suffering. Pain is inevitable; life comes with pain. Suffering is not inevitable. . . . Suffering is what happens when we struggle with our experience because of our inability to accept it.

According to Thich Nhat Hanh, "The Buddha called suffering a Holy Truth, because our suffering has the capacity of showing us the path to liberation. Embrace your suffering, and let it reveal to you the way to peace."

The third Noble Truth is: "There is a way out of suffering." Robert Thurman, one of the first Caucasian Americans to study Tibetan

70

RELIGION & MODERN CULTURE

Buddhism who received training from the Dalai Lama himself, says, "Everyone can go and become free of suffering. I see that this is possible. I became so free. It is possible for people to do it."

The fourth Noble Truth is: "The path—the way of living—brings freedom from suffering." This path has eight parts, so it is called the Eightfold Noble Path. These eight elements, which comprise the Buddhist way of living, are:

1. right understanding
2. right thought
3. right speech
4. right action
5. right livelihood
6. right effort
7. right mindfulness
8. right meditation

AMERICA CHANGES BUDDHISM—& BUDDHISM CHANGES AMERICA

When Walpola Piyananda came from Sri Lanka to teach in Los Angeles, he struggled to remain faithful to his spiritual traditions while living in this new country. Sri Lankan Buddhist monks did not drive cars, they wore traditional robes and sandals, and they would not touch a woman. Piyananda said, "I constantly faced the challenge of meeting the social customs of the U.S. head on, dealing with things that did not seem to coincide with our Buddhist monastic code of the discipline." He soon realized he would have to drive to get anywhere in Los Angeles. Western-style clothing made a lot more sense in the new climate. He learned to shake hands with women when he met them—otherwise he would seem

rude. Piyananda believes he is of greater service to Buddhism and to the United States because he has been willing to be flexible where necessary.

While North America has influenced and changed the ancient traditions of Buddhism, Buddhism has also influenced the United States. Thich Nhat Hanh and others teach what they call "Engaged Buddhism." This comes from the Bodhisattva vow, the promise taken when a man or woman is serious about the pursuit of awakening. The vow promises never to harm another creature. Socially engaged Buddhism assumes that one must not only refrain from doing harm, but also actively pursue the good of others. Buddhists in North America are involved in hospice care, comforting those who are dying. They also work in prisons, among the homeless, and in a number of peace actions and environmental causes.

FROM ENEMY TO ANGEL

In *A New Religious America*, Diana Eck relates a story she calls "a not-so-random act of kindness." She tells how, in March of 2000, a vandal broke into Temple Vietnam in Roslindale, Massachusetts, breaking windows and smashing an image of the Buddha. Police found the troublemaker, a fifteen-year-old boy named Angelo. The authorities asked the spiritual leader of the temple, Dr. Chi Nguyen (better known as Dr. Chi), if he wanted to press charges against the boy. Dr. Chi responded that instead of seeking justice by punishment, the temple would like to invite the whole community—and especially the vandal, Angelo, to a barbecue. The incident prompted them to work harder at getting to know their neighbors.

Many people came to the cookout: Anglos, Latinos, and African Americans, mixing with the Vietnamese Buddhist community. At this community gathering, Dr. Chi told Angelo, "Your name is Angelo, so I

would like you to be our temple angel-guardian. You should watch out for us and protect us like a guardian angel." Angelo was the culprit and everyone knew it—but now he had a chance to transform himself into a hero. As he told Diana Eck, "If I had known before what they were like, what I know now, I would never have done it."

Faced with an act of racially motivated vandalism, the Buddhist community in Roslindale reacted with what they would call "right understanding" and "right actions." Rather than seek punishment, they sought the welfare of their enemy. By doing so, they were able to help a young man achieve a sort of spiritual awakening.

Hinduism, like Buddhism, is an Eastern religion moving to the United States and Canada. Hindus share with Buddhists the importance of meditation. Hinduism's origin, however, is even more ancient than Buddhism's.

Chapter 5

NORTH AMERICAN HINDUISM

It is a hot summer day in May. A large group of Hindus gathers outside their new temple in suburban Boston. For many months, they have been preparing for this moment.

Building a new Hindu temple is not a small task. Priests had to select a location. Architects designed a plan for the building to suit the needs of the community. Artisans from India constructed the ornamentation for the temple. Many priests from America and India traveled to suburban Boston to prepare the temple for holy use. They built fire altars all around the temple and ceaselessly chanted holy hymns to invoke the divine into the temple. Now all of this is over, and everyone gathers around to witness the opening of the eyes of the central God in the temple, Lakshima, Goddess of wealth and blessing.

This is an important moment. When one looks into the eyes of the Gods in the temple, it is known as *Darshan*, which literally means, "seeing." When Hindus behold Darshan, they are not only looking into the eyes of the divine, but the divine is also looking at them. The first creature allowed to see Lakshima's eyes is a cow named Darling from the local dairy farm. Any Hindu will tell you they do not worship cows, but they love and respect cows as bearers of blessings. After Darling witnesses Darshan, fifteen girls in their nicest outfits see the eyes of Lakshima. Finally, all adult Hindus who have been waiting go inside the temple to look into the eyes of Lakshima.

This is a once-in-a-lifetime moment for all of them. But the opening of a new temple is only a small part of the American Hindu experience, which is continuing to grow and evolve.

HISTORY

Americans' first encounter with Hinduism was through the writings of Ralph Waldo Emerson and Henry David Thoreau. In the 1830s, Emerson got hold of a copy of the Bagavad Gita and started reading it. Later, he wrote:

> It was the first of books; it was as if an empire spoke to us, nothing small or unworthy, but large, serene, consistent, the voice of an old intelligence which in another age and climate had pondered and thus disposed of the same questions which exercise us.

Emerson's friend Thoreau brought the Bagavad Gita with him to Walden Pond. Both authors were fascinated with the ideas of Hinduism, but neither of them had ever met a real Hindu, and they did not have a full understanding of the religion.

GLOSSARY

mantras: Sacred words, chants, or sounds that are repeated during meditation to facilitate spiritual power and transformation of consciousness.

monists: Those that believe in the theory or point of view that attempts to explain everything in terms of a single principle.

polytheistic: Characterized by the belief in more than one god.

In 1893, Swami Vivekanada spoke at the World's Parliament of Religions in Chicago. He had a very welcoming audience after he spoke his first five words: "Brothers and Sisters of America." The whole building thundered in applause. Vivekanada stayed in America for two more years and set up the Vedanta Society in New York. This was the first Hindu organization to attract Americans.

The next steps to Hinduism in America came in the 1960s. First was the growth of the Hare Krishna movement, which emphasized the religious aspect of Hinduism much more than the Vedanta Society did. Although the group was small, devoted Westerners lived together, worshipped together, and performed the same rituals they would if they were in India.

The 1965 Immigration Act allowed people from Asia to come to America. As Indians entered North America, they brought with them their Hindu beliefs and deities. For some time, however, their worship was kept in the home. Then, as Hindu communities grew in the suburbs,

they began to meet at local YMCAs, and eventually, Hindus built their own temples in North America. Currently, there are more than 1.5 million Hindus living in the United States, almost all of them immigrants from India. The Canadian Council of Hindus says there are a quarter of a million followers of their religion in that nation.

BELIEFS

Hinduism is the oldest religion in the world; some estimates say it is four thousand years old. Hinduism does not have a founder, a central organization, or one holy book on which the entire religion is based. Nevertheless, Hinduism is a very complex system of thinking. Its books of scripture are the Vedas and the Upanishads. The Vedas are hymns, incantations, and rituals, while the Upanishads explain how the soul can unite with ultimate truth. The most popular religious text in Hinduism is the Bagavad Gita, a discussion between the gods Arjuna and Krishna.

Many people in the West have debated whether Hinduism is a *polytheistic* or a monotheistic religion. Hindus are *monists*; they recognize one deity, but also worship different manifestations of that one God. The supreme God is Brahman. He is not limited to any characteristics. In Hinduism's holy texts, Brahman is of a neuter (neither masculine nor feminine) gender.

Hinduism teaches its adherents to be tolerant of other religions. Perhaps the most important saying in Hinduism is, "*Ekam sat viprah bahudha vadanti*": "The truth is one, but different sages call it by different names." Hinduism teaches the oneness of truth and the oneness of the world.

A major belief in Hinduism is reincarnation, the belief that one's soul transfers after death into another body. As one lives, one accumulates *karma*, the sum of one's good and bad deeds. If one lives with pure acts and has good karma, one will be reborn into a higher form of life. If one

> *"The truth is one, but different sages call it by different names."*
> —*Universal Hindu saying*

lives doing bad deeds, and has bad karma, he will be born into a lower social class, or maybe even an animal. Whether a person has wealth, honor, or good fortune is a consequence of karma.

CAR PUJA

A *puja* is a ceremony to keep an object from bad influences and to bless it in God's name. A Hindu can perform a puja on any type of object—even a car. The puja ceremony involves many things. These can include sprinkling holy water on the object, reciting **mantras**, breaking a coconut on the object, breaking lemons and driving over them, then driving around the temple. Jennifer Polan, who participated in the ceremony, says:

> Participating in this Puja was a calming experience for me. I also was happy to share this experience with my mother, niece, and a good friend. Although I'd attended a car Puja some years ago, I came to understand this Puja more after having been the main participant myself.

This is a perfect example of an ancient Hindu tradition updated for today's world.

WHY DO THEIR GODS APPEAR THAT WAY?

Many people wonder about the appearance of the gods in Hinduism. For every one of them there is an explanation. For instance, the God Ganesha, remover of obstacles, is one of the most notable with his human-like body and head of an elephant. Why is this? According to one account, Ganesha was created by the Goddess Parvati to guard her doorway as she bathed. When Shiva, Parvati's husband, came home he asked Ganesha to let him into her room. Ganesha obeyed Parvati's wish and did not let him through. A battle began, during which Ganesha lost his head. Shiva searched for a new head for the God's body, and the first candidate he found was an elephant's head. Another reason for his elephant head is because a god that removes obstacles of all types should have the head of a powerful animal. Every god in Hinduism is rich in symbolism and meaning.

"Suppose we each one of us go with a particular pot in our hand to fetch water from a lake. . . . He who has brought the cup has water in the form of a cup, he who brought the jar, his water in the shape of a jar, and so forth. . . . So, in the case of religion, our minds are like these little pots, and each one of us is seeing God. God is like that water filling the form of the vessel. Yet He is one. He is God in every case."

—*Swami Vivekananda, founder of the Vedanta Society*

HINDUISM BECOMES MORE ESTABLISHED IN NORTH AMERICA

As we continue to move ahead to the future, surely Hinduism will continue to evolve in the United States and Canada. Most Hindu families are only in the second generation in America, and only in the past thirty years have Hindus started to feel more at home in America. One woman describes how much more fulfilling her life feels from having a temple in her neighborhood: "I moved to the U.S. in 1972. . . . There was no temple then, not really any community. I was so lonely. I used to cry every day. And now this"—she points toward an altar with an image of Krishna—"now we have a temple right here. I come every day."

American Hindus have much to face in the future, but they hope it will be a future more open and accepting of their faith. They believe it takes many generations for one's karma to reach its goals; likewise, the first generations of North American Hindus will take some time to become more comfortable in the United States and Canada.

Chapter 6

NORTH AMERICAN SANTERIA

Nestled into almost any Hispanic section of New York City are small shops called *botanicas*. Inside are images of Catholic saints, musical instruments, and lottery tickets at the front. Deeper inside the shops, one can find different herbs, potions, cauldrons, and candles. To followers of Santeria, these stores are havens for all of the needs of their religion.

One estimate puts the number of Santeria followers in New York City at 300,000. However, it is impossible to know exactly how many people follow this religion because of its secretive nature. The botanicas are one of the few signs of Santeria you can see without entering people's houses or apartments to witness their practices. Ever since its beginnings, this religion has had a shroud of secrecy.

A SECRET HISTORY

Santeria first originated among the Yoruba people in West Africa. In the sixteenth century, when the Spanish started taking slaves from West Africa to Cuba, they never realized they were planting the seeds of Santeria.

Owners did not allow slaves to practice their native religion when they got to Cuba, so the Africans adapted to new circumstances. They took each of their *Orishas*, or minor deities, and attached them to Catholic saints. For instance, if a Yoruba slave was praying to Saint Rafael in front of his masters, he was really praying to the Orisha Inle, the Orisha of medicine. The Spanish slave masters named the practice of worshipping the saints, and not God, Santeria.

After Cuba freed the slaves, these people of African descent more fully developed Santeria, combining old Yoruba beliefs with elements of Spanish culture. Even though the slaves were free now, they kept their religion secret, because they knew whites would think their religion was odd and would persecute them.

Santeria first made its way to America through the slave trade. Later, whenever groups of Cubans (as well as other Caribbean Islanders) immigrated to America, some of them brought their religion with them.

GLOSSARY

personifications: Embodiments or perfect examples of something.

FIVE LEVELS OF POWER

Santeria does not have one book of sacred teachings. Instead, it is a faith built on traditions that are passed on orally.

The Santeria system of belief has five levels of power: First is Olodumare (also known as Olorun), the supreme God, the "owner of heaven" who created the world. Second in importance are the Orishas, who are helpers of Olodumare and do his bidding. They could be compared to angels in Christianity, although they have much more prominence than angels do in the Bible. Each Santerian has an Orisha who guides her in life and watches over her, and each Orisha represents a saint, a principle, a number, color, dance posture, and emblem. Many think the saints who represent the Orishas are just disguises for Yoruba ancient gods, but they mean more than that; according to Santeria, the saints are *personifications* in the Catholic world of the Orishas. The other three levels of power are humans, human ancestors, and then plants, animals, and spiritual tools.

Santerians use many rituals to encounter the Orishas. The two most controversial ones are animal sacrifice and possession.

"Then I think the Orisha must be something like wind, it comes towards you like a wind and embraces you."

—*Candomble woman describing her trance*

ANIMAL SACRIFICE

Many American groups have protested the act of animal sacrifice. Santerians answer that animal sacrifices are only done for special occasions—when someone is in great need, when a person is sick, or when someone is going through something life threatening. Santerians believe a person gains general well-being through sacrifices to the Orishas, and they give the blood of the sacrificed animal to the Orisha. Sacrifices are done humanely, with as little pain for the animal as possible. Practitioners point out to those who are angered by animal sacrifice that most Americans eat the meat of animals that have been slaughtered less humanely, and for a cause that is not sacred to them.

Public outcry reached its highest level when the Santerian Church of Lukumi Babalu Aye went to court in 1992 for its animal sacrifices. The lawsuit stated that the church had broken the town of Hialeah, Florida's, ordinance that made it illegal to "unnecessarily kill, torment, torture, or mutilate an animal in a public or private ritual or ceremony not for the primary purpose of food consumption." The law seemed created to stop Santerian practices of religion. The founder of the church, Ernesto Pichardo, fought the ordinance as a violation of Santerians' First Amendment rights. The case went all the way to the Supreme Court, which, in 1993, ruled in favor of the Santerians.

WHAT TO CALL IT

There is some question as to what to call the religion of Santeria. Santeria is its common and popular name, but the literal Spanish translation means "the way of the saints." A name that is sometimes used today is "Regla de Ocha" or "rule of the Orisha." *Lukumi* is yet another word, related to a Yoruba word meaning "friend" that refers to both the religion and its followers.

POSSESSION

Santerians believe when a person becomes possessed he leaves his soul temporarily and the soul of the Orisha comes inside of him. This experience is literally the invisible world manifested into the visible. One can see, talk to, and hear the Orisha. The possession ceremony involves drumming, and each Orisha has its own drumbeat and dance.

A woman going through the experience of possession for the Brazilian religion Candomble, which is very similar to Santeria, describes her experience:

"This is Mother Nature's religion."
—*Santero Steve Quintana*

I feel this way, that the Orisha wants to get me, my legs tremble, something reaches me and takes over my heart, my head grows, I see the blue light, I look for someone to grab but I can't find anyone, and then I can't see anyone anymore. Then everything happens and I don't see. Then I think the Orisha must be something like wind, it comes towards you like a wind and embraces you. Like a shock in my heart, my heart beats as fast as the lead drum plays, my head grows, and it seems I see a blue light ahead of me and a hole appears in the middle of the room. Then I want to run, grab someone, but people seem far away, out of reach. Then I don't see anyone anymore.

HIDDEN IN THE CULTURE

Despite its secretive nature, Santeria has made some minor marks on American popular culture, even though most people do not know it. According to the Web site WorldWide Religion News, when Desi Arnaz banged his bongo drums and yelled "Babalu!" in the 1950s sitcom *I Love Lucy*, he was doing so in praise of the Orisha Babalu Aye. Gloria Estefan pays tribute to Santeria with her drumbeats and chants. Some readers might be familiar with the song "Santeria" by Sublime, with the first line, "I don't practice Santeria, I ain't got no crystal ball."

RELIGION & MODERN CULTURE

THE FUTURE

Americans are growing more and more interested in ancient tribal alternative religions such as Santeria. Both black and Hispanic minorities who do not practice the religion may be intrigued and want to explore their religious roots. Whites have shown a growing curiosity in Santeria as well, and a few Santeria leaders have started to make their religion more visible and open to America. Boston *santero* (or priest) Steve Quintana says:

> We're trying to expose the religion. . . . It's been hidden for many years. We're trying to make sure people understand the religion itself. They think we are doing evil or wrong to others. We are not. This is Mother Nature's religion.

Chapter 7

OTHER FAITHS IN THE UNITED STATES & CANADA

Jessica Klein grew up in a devout Christian home, but she had many doubts about her parents' faith. She always had questions about who went to heaven, how a loving God could send people to hell, and why her parents believed the Bible was true. She decided she was morally opposed to organized religion. When she married, her lack of faith in traditional religions was no problem to her husband, who was an agnostic. After they had children, however, they realized a need for some form of open-minded religion. Klein says, "The dilemma became painfully clear: how would we raise a child to learn about our Christian backgrounds, understand my religious pluralism, accept my husband's agnostic beliefs, and find this all in an open-minded, non-traditional congregation?" Unitarian Universalism provided for all these needs.

Klein states:

I knew that I had come home. The juxtaposition where this majestic, historical church with beautiful stained glass windows and gardens in the courtyard met the liberal, thought-provoking, and frequently controversial sermons of our minister, Drew, swept me off my feet. Our son was dedicated at First Unitarian this past Mother's Day.

UNITARIAN UNIVERSALISTS

Unitarian Universalism is not a newcomer to America's shores. It has been here since the time of the American Revolution. Benjamin Franklin was a Unitarian Universalist, and so were Thomas Jefferson and Paul Revere. Many famous literary artists were and are Unitarian Universalists, including Henry David Thoreau, e. e. cummings, Kurt Vonnegut, and Sylvia Plath.

There are 629,000 Unitarian Universalists in the United States today, while Canada claims 18,500 Unitarians. In the United States, Unitarians are growing in number, reporting a 25 percent increase in membership between 1990 and 2001. This is unusual for a group with such a long history in America.

Unitarians are liberal and open in their beliefs. Tolerance is their most important belief. They respect all religions. A Buddhist could join the Unitarian Universalist Church; so could a Christian, Jew, or Hindu. The emphasis in Unitarian Universalism is on the individual rather than the group: the individual can decide what is true for herself. Unitarian John Sias says:

GLOSSARY

genocide: The deliberate and systematic destruction of a racial, political, or cultural group.

indigenous: Native to an area.

Most of us do not believe in a supernatural, supreme being who can directly intervene in and alter human life or the mechanism of the natural world. Many believe in a spirit of life or a power within themselves, which some choose to call God.

Unitarians work hard to accept people who are traditionally left out or marginalized by traditional religions—women, minorities, and homosexuals. Many women, minorities, and homosexuals are even in clergy positions in the Unitarian Universalist Church. Unitarian Universalists are strong believers in diversity of all sorts.

Almost all members of the Unitarian Universalist Church are politically liberal people who believe in social change and social justice. A few issues that Unitarian Universalists are most active in are environmentalism, feminism, same-sex marriage, and stopping atrocities abroad. An example of activism in the Unitarian Universalist Associa-

RELIGION & MODERN CULTURE

"Universalists are often asked where they stand. The only true answer to give to this question is that we do not stand at all, we move."
—*L. B. Fisher*

tion is the August 2004 arrest of the president of the Unitarian Universalist Church at a protest against the **genocide** in Sudan. In his sermon, the Reverend William Sinkford said, "This is a day of conscience. We have come together to stand in solidarity with both the suffering and the possibility that is represented in a part of the world that is far away from our own homes." Joking about his past activism, he added, "It's been too long since I've been arrested."

The Unitarian Church often alters itself to fit different religious traditions as they change. An example of this occurred in 1995 when the church expanded its official beliefs to encompass "Spiritual teachings of earth-centered traditions which celebrate the sacred circle of life and instruct us to live in harmony with the rhythms of nature," thereby including members of earth-centered and Native American religions.

WICCAN/PAGAN/DRUID

Wicca, the most popular form of a broader movement known as Paganism, may be North America's fastest-growing religion. Many Wiccans are hesitant to tell others about their religion because they fear misunderstanding. Therefore, estimates of Wiccan numbers vary greatly, from a low guess of 200,000 to the high guess of 5 million in North America today. A recent attempt to determine numbers based on results of the American Religious Identification Survey came up with an estimated 750,000 practitioners in the United States and 40,000 in

Canada. Those numbers make Wicca North America's seventh-largest religion. Whatever the numbers are, all religious scholars agree that Wicca is growing rapidly.

"Wicca" (pronounced "wik-ah") is an ancient Anglo-Saxon term for magic or sorcery. It is also the root word for witchcraft. Wicca is a specific form of a broader set of beliefs known as Paganism. Paganism is the worship of goddesses and gods, as opposed to the one God of Christianity, Judaism, and Islam. Paganism aims to restart ancient traditions that ended, or came close to ending, in centuries past. Forms of Paganism distinct from Wicca include Druidism (the worship of ancient Celtic deities), Asatru (worship of the ancient Norse deities), Egyptian Paganism, Greco-Roman Paganism, the Women's Spirituality Movement, and Unitarian Universalist Pagans (affiliated with churches of that name). Its followers often refer to Wicca as "the Craft."

The Goddess, the Great Mother, is the most important being in Wicca. The practice of Magick is also an important part of the Craft. Aleister Crowley, a pioneer of modern witchcraft, defined Magick as "the ability to make changes in physical reality by nonphysical means, especially by sheer willpower." Magick usually involves ritual objects such as a magic circle, a sacred knife, or a wand. Wiccans believe Magick is controlled by the "Threefold Law of Return." This law states that any Magick directed toward others will return to its originator three times as strongly.

Wiccans strongly deny any connection with Satanism. On the Witches' Voice Web site, Dana Corby writes, "Just like Christian parents, we are especially concerned about literature which links Witchcraft and Satanism. We agree with them that Satanism is not anything we want our children involved in; we just adamantly contend that it has nothing to do with us."

RELIGION & MODERN CULTURE

BAHA'I

The Baha'i faith is also growing rapidly in North America today. Between 1990 and 2001, Baha'i membership in the United States increased from 28,000 to 84,000, an amazing 200 percent increase in a single decade.

According to the New Religious Movements Web site of the University of Virginia:

> The Baha'i Faith believes there is only one God. . . . He is revealed throughout history by a number of divine Messengers. These Messengers include Zoroaster, Moses, Buddha, Jesus, Krishna, and Muhammad. The latest of these divine Messengers was Baha'u'llah whose role, along with past Messengers, was to educate humanity. The Baha'i believe that God continually sends Messengers and the past prophets are all manifestations of the same spirit.

TRADITIONAL SPIRITUAL BELIEFS OF THE FIRST NATIONS

Many of the religious beliefs discussed in this book—such as Hinduism, Buddhism, and Baha'i—are recent arrivals on the North American religious scene. Others, such as Christianity and Judaism, came with those

from Europe who colonized this continent. Yet other religions, such as Santeria and Islam, came with Africans whom the Europeans enslaved and forced to build their empires in the Americas.

Before all of these religions came to the New World, *indigenous* people followed hundreds of different spiritual beliefs. From the Arctic Circle in the north, to the steaming forests of Central America, Natives of the Americas followed their own sacred ways. Spiritual rituals varied greatly—from the healing societies of the Haudenosaunee in the Northeast woodlands, to the Kachina dancers of the Hopis in the south-western desert, to the huge and elegant pyramids dedicated to the Sun God in Mexico and Guatemala.

Although extremely diverse, the First Nations throughout Canada and the United States hold some beliefs in common. Most traditional Native people revere Mother Earth and show great respect for natural forces. In addition, Native Americans respect their ancestors, and they believe deceased ancestors are still present and active in their lives. Their beliefs also have common elements of spiritual practice, such as drumming and dancing in a circle. Native languages often lacked words for "religion" because they did not separate "religion" from "ordinary life." Indigenous people who follow traditional ways regard all of life as sacred.

For centuries, Canadian and U.S. governments attempted to destroy traditional Native beliefs. Government agents sent American Indian children to boarding schools and punished them for practicing their cultures. Missionaries taught that traditional Native spirituality was "devilish," and government agencies forbade such essential spiritual practices as the Sun Dance in the Great Plains states and the Potlatch ceremonies on the Northwest Coast.

Finally, in the 1960s and 1970s, First Nations people were able to reassert their rights to spiritual expression. After centuries of targeted discrimination, North American Indians could begin to enjoy the same freedom of religion that other North Americans had long experienced. As a result, indigenous people throughout the Americas are returning

to the beliefs and ceremonies of their ancestors. At the same time, they continue to fight for their full religious rights, including protection of sacred sites and plants.

In the United States in 2001, more than 100,000 First Nations peoples identified themselves as following some form of "Native American Religion." Again, surveys of spiritual belief are often inaccurate, and there are several reasons to believe these numbers are lower than reality. Nevertheless, they do indicate an increase of more than 100 percent in a decade. In Canada in 2001, some thirty thousand people indicated they follow traditional Native spiritual ways. That is an increase of 175 percent in a decade.

"Wisdom comes only when you stop looking for it and live the life the Creator intended for you"

—*Hopi Proverb*

A Northern Cheyenne man witnessed a buffalo dance ritual conducted near the gateway of Yellowstone National Park. Because of government restrictions, Native Americans had not done this dance in public for more than a century. His grandson also watched the ritual. After the ceremony, his grandson said, "Grandpa, awesome!" The grandfather concluded, "I have a very good feeling that I have someone who . . . will follow the Indian ways."

In the midst of North America's religious diversity, there are still many who follow the spiritual practices passed down from their ancestors, from a time before Europeans, Africans, and Asians arrived on the continent.

CONCLUSION

In the past, many regarded the United States and Canada as Judeo-Christian nations. In the twenty-first century, however, both nations are more akin to a spiritual smorgasbord, serving a great variety of differing spiritual beliefs. This book has described the ten most common spiritual beliefs in North America today. However, these are only a handful of the hundreds of different varieties of faith in the United States and Canada. In coming years, it is likely there will be even greater spiritual diversity.

In order for the United States and Canada to prosper, it will be important for citizens to embrace true religious pluralism. In a pluralistic society, each person will be free to follow her own spiritual beliefs with pride and without compromise—while understanding and appreciating the differing beliefs of her neighbors.

107

FURTHER READING

108

Ali, Abdullah Yusuf. *The Meaning of the Holy Qur'an*. Beltsville, Md.: Amana Publications, 1999.

Eck, Diana L. *A New Religious America*. San Francisco: Harper Collins, 2001.

Elias, Jamal J. *The Pocket Idiot's Guide to Islam*. Indianapolis, Ind.: Alpha, 2003.

Gonzalez-Wippler, Migene. *Santeria: Faith, Rites, Magic*. St. Paul, Minn.: Llewellyn, 1994.

Hanh, Thich Nhat. *Living Buddha, Living Christ*. New York: Putnam, 1995.

Magida, Arthur, and Stuart Matlins. *How to Be a Perfect Stranger: A Guide to Etiquette in Other People's Religious Ceremonies*. Woodstock, Vt.: Jewish Lights Publishing, 1995.

Maguire, Jack. *Essential Buddhism*. New York: Simon & Schuster, 2001.

McIntosh, Kenneth. *People of Faith and Vision: The Latino Religious Experience*. Philadelphia: Mason Crest, 2005.

McIntosh, Kenneth. *Women in North America's Religious World*. Philadelphia: Mason Crest, 2005.

Robinson, Jonathan. *The Complete Idiot's Guide to Awakening Your Spirituality*. Indianapolis, Ind.: Alpha, 2000.

FOR MORE INFORMATION

Adherents.com
www.adherents.com

Beliefnet
www.beliefnet.com

Christianity Today
www.christianitytoday.com

Hinduism Online
www.himalayanacademy.com

Islam Online
www.islamonline.net

Judaism 101
www.jewfaq.org

New Religious Movements
religiousmovements.lib.virginia

Plum Village Meditation Center
(Thich Nhat Hanh's official Web
site)
www.plumvillage.org

Religious Tolerance.org
www.religioustolerance.org

The Witches' Voice
www.witchvox.com

Unitarian Universalist
Association
www.uaa.org

Publisher's note:
The Web sites listed on this page were active at the time of publication. The publisher is not responsible for Web sites that have changed
their addresses or discontinued operation since the date of publication.
The publisher will review and update the Web-site list upon each
reprint..

109

110   INDEX

PICTURE CREDITS

The illustrations in RELIGION AND MODERN CULTURE are photo montages made by Dianne Hodack. They are a combination of her original mixed-media paintings and collages, the photography of Benjamin Stewart, various historical public-domain artwork, and other royalty-free photography collections.

Paintings by the following artists were used on the following pages:

Elio Vilva, Cuban Art Space, Center for Cuban Studies, New York, N.Y.: pp. 91, 92

Luis Rodriguez, Cuban Art Space, Center for Cuban Studies, New York, N.Y.: pp. 84, 85, 110, 111

AUTHORS: Kenneth McIntosh is a freelance writer living in Flagstaff, Arizona, with his wife Marsha and their two children—along with two cats and a dog. He has a bachelor's degree in English and a master's degree in theology. He is the author of more than a dozen books, including *Women in North America's Religious World* and *People of Faith and Vision: The Latino Religious Experience*. He formerly spent a decade teaching junior high in inner-city Los Angeles, and another decade serving as an ordained minister. He enjoys hiking, boogie boarding, and vintage Volkswagens. This book was written with the help of his son, Jonathan McIntosh, who enjoys reading, writing, and making music.

CONSULTANT: Dr. Marcus J. Borg is the Hundere Distinguished Professor of Religion and Culture in the Philosophy Department at Oregon State University. Dr. Borg is past president of the Anglican Association of Biblical Scholars. Internationally known as a biblical and Jesus scholar, the *New York Times* called him "a leading figure among this generation of Jesus scholars." He is the author of twelve books, which have been translated into eight languages. Among them are *The Heart of Christianity: Rediscovering a Life of Faith* (2003) and *Meeting Jesus Again for the First Time* (1994), the best-selling book by a contemporary Jesus scholar.

CONSULTANT: Dr. Robert K. Johnston is Professor of Theology and Culture at Fuller Theological Seminary in Pasadena, California, having served previously as Provost of North Park University and as a faculty member of Western Kentucky University. The author or editor of thirteen books and twenty-five book chapters (including *The Christian at Play*, 1983; *The Variety of American Evangelicalism*, 1991; *Reel Spirituality: Theology and Film in Dialogue*, 2000; *Life Is Not Work/Work Is Not Life: Simple Reminders for Finding Balance in a 24/7 World*, 2000; *Finding God in the Movies: 33 Films of Reel Faith*, 2004; and *Useless Beauty: Ecclesiastes Through the Lens of Contemporary Film*, 2004), Johnston is the immediate past president of the American Theological Society, an ordained Protestant minister, and an avid bodysurfer.